Bread Machine Cookbook UK 2022

The Ultimate Bread Making Guide for Beginners with Easy, Delicious and Hands-Off Recipes

Author: Sarah Williams

Legal Notice:

Copyright 2022 by Sarah Williams - All rights reserved.

This document is geared towards providing exact and reliable information regarding the topic and issue covered. The publication is sold on the idea that the publisher is not required to render an accounting, officially permitted, or otherwise, qualified services. If advice is necessary, legal or professional, a practiced individual in the profession should be ordered.

From a Declaration of Principles which was accepted and approved equally by a Committee of the American Bar Association and a Committee of Publishers and Associations.

Legal Notes:

In no way is it legal to reproduce, duplicate, or transmit any part of this document by either electronic means or in printed format. Recording of this publication is strictly prohibited and any storage of this document is not allowed unless with written permission from the publisher. All rights reserved.

The information provided herein is stated to be truthful and consistent, in that any liability, in terms of inattention or otherwise, by any usage or abuse of any policies, processes, or directions contained within is the solitary and utter responsibility of the recipient reader. Under no circumstances will any legal responsibility or blame be held against the publisher for any reparation, damages, or monetary loss due to the information herein, either directly or indirectly. Respective authors own all copyrights not held by the publisher.

Disclaimer Notice:

The information herein is offered for informational purposes solely and is universal as so. The presentation of the information is without a contract or any type of guarantee assurance. Readers acknowledge that the author is not engaging in the rendering of legal, financial, medical or professional advice. Please consult a licensed professional before attempting any techniques outlined in this book.

By continuing with this book, readers agree that the author is under no circumstances responsible for any losses, indirect or direct, that are incurred as a result of the information presented in this document, including, but not limited to inaccuracies, omissions and errors.

The trademarks that are used are without any consent, and the publication of the trademark is without permission or backing by the trademark owner. All trademarks and brands within this book are for clarifying purposes only and are the owned by the owners themselves, not affiliated with this document.

Table of Contents

Sweet Bread Recipes 7
- **Simple White Bread** 8
- **Buttered White Bread** 9
- **Simple Whole-Wheat Bread** 10
- **Yoghurt Whole-Wheat Bread** 11
- **Basic Whole-Wheat Bread** 12
- **Milky Whole-Wheat Bread** 13
- **Spelt Bread** 14
- **Quinoa Bread** 15
- **Flaxseed Bread** 16
- **Oats Bread** 17
- **Courgette Lemon Bread** 18
- **Cinnamon Bread** 19
- **Dark Rye Bread** 20
- **Applesauce Raisin Bread** 21
- **Honey Molasses Quinoa Bread** 22
- **Raisin Caraway bread** 23
- **Sourdough Bread** 24
- **Challah Bread** 25
- **Millet & Cornmeal Bread** 26
- **Rice Flour Bread** 27
- **Multi-Grain Cereal Bread** 28
- **Mixed Seeds Bread** 29
- **Date & Almond Bread** 30
- **Walnut Bread** 31
- **Mango Bread** 32
- **Banana Oat Bread** 33
- **Apple Bread** 34
- **Blueberry Bread** 35

Lemon Bread	36
Carrot Bread	37
Courgette Raisin Bread	38
Two Sugars Bread	39
Molasses Whole-Wheat Bread	40
Honey Bread	41
Maple Bread	42
Peanut Butter Jelly Bread	43
Raisin Bread	44
Currant Bread	45
Pineapple Bread	46
Pumpkin Bread	47
Pumpkin Cranberry Bread	48
Banana Pecans Bread	49
Cranberry Bread	50
Cranberry Orange Bread	51
Raspberry Bread	52
Orange Honey Bread	53
Banana Chocolate Bread	54
Sweet Potato Bread	55
Gingerbread	56
Mustard Bread	57
Star Anise Bread	58
Orange Bread Cake	59
Chocolate Bread Cake	60
Chocolate Chip Bread	61
Mocha Bread	62
Sunflower Seed Oat Bread	63
Ciabatta Bread	64
Savory Bread Recipes	**65**

Mustard Curry Bread	66
Mustard Dill Bread	67
Tomato Rosemary Bread	68
Potato Bread	69
Parmesan Parsley Bread	70
Pepperoni Bread	71
Caramelized Onion Bread	72
Herbed Garlic Bread	73
Cheddar Bread	74
Mixed Herbs Bread	75
Chives Bread	76
Rosemary Bread	77
Olives Bread	78
Celery Bread	79
Tomato & Onion Bread	80
Parmesan Garlic Bread	81
Cheddar & Parmesan Bread	82
Ricotta Bread	83
Cheddar Green Onion Bread	84
Feta Olives Bread	85
Buns, Breadsticks & Muffins Recipes	86
Simple Buns	87
Whole-Wheat Buns	88
Milky Buns	89
Buttered Buns	90
Cinnamon Buns	91
Honey Buns	92
Cherries Buns	93
Brioche Buns	94
Cheddar & Cream Buns	95

Swiss Cheese Buns	96
Simple Breadsticks	97
Whole-Wheat Breadsticks	98
Sesame Seed Breadsticks	99
Brown Sugar Breadsticks	100
Buttered Breadsticks	101
Honey Breadsticks	102
Italian Seasoning Breadsticks	103
Basil Parmesan Breadsticks	104
Monterrey Jack Breadsticks	105
Prosciutto Breadsticks	106
Milk Powder English Muffins	107
Honey English Muffins	108
Milky English Muffins	109
Raisin English Muffins	110
Buttermilk Muffins	111
Index	112

Sweet Bread Recipes

Simple White Bread

Servings|12   Time|3¼ hours
Nutritional Content (per serving):
Cal| 170   Fat| 2.3g   Protein| 4.5g   Carbs| 32.4g   Fibre| 1.1g

Ingredients:

- Water (255 millilitres, lukewarm)
- Bread flour (440 grams)
- Salt (5 grams)
- Large egg (1, beaten)
- Vegetable oil (20 millilitres)
- Instant yeast (7 grams)

Directions:

1. Place all ingredients in the baking pan of bread machine in the order recommended by manufacturer.
2. Place the baking pan in bread machine and close with lid.
3. Select "Basic" setting.
4. Press start button.
5. Carefully remove the baking pan from machine and then invert the bread loaf onto a wire rack to cool completely before slicing.
6. Cut the bread loaf into desired-sized slices and serve.

Buttered White Bread

Servings|12   Time|4 hours 5 minutes

Nutritional Content (per serving):

Cal| 181   Fat| 2.4g   Protein| 5.2g   Carbs| 33.8g   Fibre| 5.2g

Ingredients:

- Water (330 millilitres, lukewarm)
- White sugar (15 grams)
- White flour (490 grams)
- Active dry yeast (3 grams)
- Dry milk powder (30 grams)
- Salt (5 grams)
- Unsalted butter (30 grams, softened)

Directions:

1. Place all ingredients in the baking pan of bread machine in the order recommended by manufacturer.
2. Place the baking pan in bread machine and close with lid.
3. Select "Basic" setting.
4. Press start button.
5. Carefully remove the baking pan from machine and then invert the bread loaf onto a wire rack to cool completely before slicing.
6. Cut the bread loaf into desired-sized slices and serve.

Simple Whole-Wheat Bread

Servings|12   Time|3 hours 5 minutes

Nutritional Content (per serving):

Cal| 150   Fat| 1.7g   Protein| 4.8g   Carbs| 28.6g   Fibre| 1.2g

Ingredients:

- Active dry yeast (4½ grams)
- Salt (7½ grams)
- Dry milk powder (25 grams)
- Water (300 millilitres, warm)
- Whole-wheat flour (390 grams)
- White sugar (25 grams)
- Margarine (20 grams)

Directions:

1. Place all ingredients in the baking pan of bread machine in the order recommended by manufacturer.
2. Place the baking pan in bread machine and close with lid.
3. Select "Whole Wheat" setting.
4. Press start button.
5. Carefully remove the baking pan from machine and then invert the bread loaf onto a wire rack to cool completely before slicing.
6. Cut the bread loaf into desired-sized slices and serve.

Yoghurt Whole-Wheat Bread

Servings|12   Time|3 hours 25 minutes

Nutritional Content (per serving):

Cal| 194   Fat| 3.7g   Protein| 5.4g   Carbs| 34.2g   Fibre| 1.1g

Ingredients:

- Whole-wheat flour (455 grams)
- Salt (2½ grams)
- Plain yoghurt (125 grams)
- Instant yeast (4½ grams)
- White sugar (40 grams)
- Whole milk (255 millilitres)
- Unsalted butter (40 grams, softened)

Directions:

1. Place all ingredients in the baking pan of bread machine in the order recommended by manufacturer.
2. Place the baking pan in bread machine and close with lid.
3. Select "Basic" setting and then "Regular Crust".
4. Press start button.
5. Carefully remove the baking pan from machine and then invert the bread loaf onto a wire rack to cool completely before slicing.
6. Cut the bread loaf into desired-sized slices and serve.

Basic Whole-Wheat Bread

Servings|12   Time|4 hours 5 minutes

Nutritional Content (per serving):

Cal| 185   Fat| 2.7g   Protein| 4.6g   Carbs| 34.8g   Fibre| 1.2g

Ingredients:

- Water (360 millilitres, warm)
- White sugar (20 grams)
- Whole-wheat flour (520 grams)
- Vegetable oil (30 millilitres)
- Salt (2½ grams)
- Instant yeast (3 grams)

Directions:

1. Place all ingredients in the baking pan of bread machine in the order recommended by manufacturer.
2. Place the baking pan in bread machine and close with lid.
3. Select "Whole Wheat" setting.
4. Press start button.
5. Carefully remove the baking pan from machine and then invert the bread loaf onto a wire rack to cool completely before slicing.
6. Cut the bread loaf into desired-sized slices and serve.

Milky Whole-Wheat Bread

Servings|12   Time|3 hours 5 minutes

Nutritional Content (per serving):

Cal| 225   Fat| 4.6g   Protein| 6.4g   Carbs| 34.8g   Fibre| 0.7g

Ingredients:

- Whole milk (360 millilitres, lukewarm)
- Whole-wheat flour (260 grams)
- Bread flour (270 grams)
- Bread machine yeast (7½ grams)
- Unsalted butter (55 grams, sliced and softened)
- Brown sugar (50 grams)
- Salt (2½ grams)

Directions:

1. Place all ingredients in the baking pan of bread machine in the order recommended by manufacturer.
2. Place the baking pan in bread machine and close with lid.
3. Select "Basic" setting.
4. Press start button.
5. Carefully remove the baking pan from machine and then invert the bread loaf onto a wire rack to cool completely before slicing.
6. Cut the bread loaf into desired-sized slices and serve.

Spelt Bread

Servings|12   Time|2 hours 5 minutes

Nutritional Content (per serving):

Cal| 166   Fat| 3.5g   Protein| 6g   Carbs| 29.9g   Fibre| 4.7g

Ingredients:

- Soy milk (300 millilitres)
- Spelt flour (430 grams)
- Salt (5 grams)
- Canola oil (30 millilitres)
- White sugar (25 grams)
- Active dry yeast (7 grams)

Directions:

1. Place all ingredients in the baking pan of bread machine in the order recommended by manufacturer.
2. Place the baking pan in bread machine and close with lid.
3. Select "Quick White Bread" setting.
4. Press start button.
5. Carefully remove the baking pan from machine and then invert the bread loaf onto a wire rack to cool completely before slicing.
6. Cut the bread loaf into desired-sized slices and serve.

Quinoa Bread

Servings|8   Time|4 hours 5 minutes

Nutritional Content (per serving):

Cal| 97   Fat| 8.2g   Protein| 4.3g   Carbs| 26.9g   Fibre| 1.8g

Ingredients:

- Almond milk (200 millilitres)
- White sugar (10 grams)
- Quinoa flour (45 grams)
- Bread machine yeast (3 grams)
- Unsalted butter (15 grams)
- Salt (5 grams)
- White flour (215 grams)

Directions:

1. Place all ingredients in the baking pan of bread machine in the order recommended by manufacturer.
2. Place the baking pan in bread machine and close with lid.
3. Select "Sweet Bread" setting and then "Light Crust".
4. Press start button.
5. Carefully remove the baking pan from machine and then invert the bread loaf onto a wire rack to cool completely before slicing.
6. Cut the bread loaf into desired-sized slices and serve.

Flaxseed Bread

Servings|10   Time|3 hours 5 minutes

Nutritional Content (per serving):

Cal| 85   Fat| 2.9g   Protein| 9.1g   Carbs| 5.1g   Fibre| 1.1g

Ingredients:

- Water (120 millilitres)
- Unsalted butter (15 grams, softened)
- Ground flaxseeds (30 grams)
- Soy flour (20 grams)
- Egg (1, beaten)
- Splenda (15 grams)
- Vital wheat gluten (90 grams)
- Dry yeast (3 grams)

Directions:

1. Place all ingredients in the baking pan of bread machine in the order recommended by manufacturer.
2. Place the baking pan in bread machine and close with lid.
3. Select "Light Browning "setting.
4. Press start button.
5. Carefully remove the baking pan from machine and then invert the bread loaf onto a wire rack to cool completely before slicing.
6. Cut the bread loaf into desired-sized slices and serve.

Oats Bread

Servings|12   Time|3 hours 5 minutes

Nutritional Content (per serving):

Cal| 140   Fat| 2g   Protcin| 3.7g   Carbs| 26.7g   Fibre| 1.4g

Ingredients:

- Water (240 millilitres)
- Unsalted butter (20 grams, softened)
- Bread flour (320 grams)
- Active dry yeast (7 grams)
- Honey (40 grams)
- Quick-cooking oats (60 grams)
- Salt (5 grams)

Directions:

1. Place all ingredients in the baking pan of bread machine in the order recommended by manufacturer.
2. Place the baking pan in bread machine and close with lid.
3. Select "White Bread" setting.
4. Press start button.
5. Carefully remove the baking pan from machine and then invert the bread loaf onto a wire rack to cool completely before slicing.
6. Cut the bread loaf into desired-sized slices and serve.

Courgette Lemon Bread

Servings|10   Time|4 hours 10 minutes

Nutritional Content (per serving):

Cal| 116   Fat| 0.3g   Protein| 3.7g   Carbs| 24.4g   Fibre| 1.2g

Ingredients:

- Unsweetened applesauce (125 grams)
- White sugar (10 grams)
- Lemon zest (5 grams, finely grated)
- Active dry yeast (6 grams)
- Courgette (70 grams, grated)
- Bread flour (270 grams)
- Ground cinnamon (1½ grams)
- Dry milk powder (15 grams)
- Salt (5 grams)
- Water (120 millilitres)

Directions:

1. Place all ingredients in the baking pan of bread machine in the order recommended by manufacturer.
2. Place the baking pan in bread machine and close with lid.
3. Select "Basic" setting.
4. Press start button.
5. Carefully remove the baking pan from machine and then invert the bread loaf onto a wire rack to cool completely before slicing.
6. Cut the bread loaf into desired-sized slices and serve.

Cinnamon Bread

Servings|10   Time|3 hours 10 minutes

Nutritional Content (per serving):

Cal| 246   Fat| 5.9g   Protein| 5.8g   Carbs| 42.8g   Fibre| 1.5g

Ingredients:

- Whole milk (240 millilitres)
- Large egg (1, beaten)
- White sugar (100 grams)
- Ground cinnamon (5 grams)
- Active dry yeast (6 grams)
- Unsalted butter (55 grams, softened)
- Bread flour (405 grams)
- Salt (2½ grams)

Directions:

1. Place all ingredients in the baking pan of bread machine in the order recommended by manufacturer.
2. Place the baking pan in bread machine and close with lid.
3. Select "White Bread" setting.
4. Press start button.
5. Carefully remove the baking pan from machine and then invert the bread loaf onto a wire rack to cool completely before slicing.
6. Cut the bread loaf into desired-sized slices and serve.

Dark Rye Bread

Servings|12   Time|4 hours 5 minutes

Nutritional Content (per serving):

Cal| 169   Fat| 2.3g   Protein| 5g   Carbs| 33.4g   Fibre| 4g

Ingredients:

- Water (360 millilitres)
- Corn syrup (40 grams)
- Margarine (20 grams, softened)
- Rye flour (120 grams)
- Brown sugar (10 grams)
- Instant coffee granules (5 grams)
- Apple cider vinegar (30 millilitres)
- Bread flour (340 grams)
- Salt (5 grams)
- Cocoa powder (20 grams)
- Caraway seeds (10 grams)
- Active dry yeast (6 grams)

Directions:

1. Place all ingredients in the baking pan of bread machine in the order recommended by manufacturer.
2. Place the baking pan in bread machine and close with lid.
3. Select "Whole Wheat" setting.
4. Press start button.
5. Carefully remove the baking pan from machine and then invert the bread loaf onto a wire rack to cool completely before slicing.
6. Cut the bread loaf into desired-sized slices and serve.

Applesauce Raisin Bread

Servings|12   Time|3¼ hours

Nutritional Content (per serving):

Cal| 177   Fat| 2.7g   Protein| 4.2g   Carbs| 34.3g   Fibre| 1.8g

Ingredients:

- Water (150 millilitres)
- Unsalted butter (30 grams)
- Bread flour (375 grams)
- Brown sugar (20 grams)
- Ground cinnamon (5 grams)
- Raisins (75 grams)
- Unsweetened applesauce (80 grams)
- Dry milk powder (25 grams)
- Salt (7½ grams)
- Instant yeast (4½ grams)

Directions:

1. Place all ingredients except for raisins in the baking pan of bread machine in the order recommended by manufacturer.
2. Place the baking pan in bread machine and close with lid.
3. Select "Basic" setting.
4. Press start button.
5. Wait for bread machine to beep before adding the raisins.
6. Carefully remove the baking pan from machine and then invert the bread loaf onto a wire rack to cool completely before slicing.
7. Cut the bread loaf into desired-sized slices and serve.

Honey Molasses Quinoa Bread

Servings|20   Time|3 hours 55 minutes

Nutritional Content (per serving):

Cal| 150   Fat| 3.6g   Protein| 4.3g   Carbs| 24.9g   Fibre| 1.2g

Ingredients:

- Water (240 millilitres)
- Honey (20 grams)
- Molasses (20 grams)
- Bread flour (315 grams)
- Salt (2½ grams)
- Olive oil (60 millilitres)
- Quinoa (185 grams, cooked)
- Whole-wheat flour (325 grams)
- Vital wheat gluten (8 grams)
- Active dry yeast (6 grams)

Directions:

1. Place all ingredients in the baking pan of bread machine in the order recommended by manufacturer.
2. Place the baking pan in bread machine and close with lid.
3. Select "Whole Wheat" setting.
4. Press start button.
5. Carefully remove the baking pan from machine and then invert the bread loaf onto a wire rack to cool completely before slicing.
6. Cut the bread loaf into desired-sized slices and serve.

Raisin Caraway bread

Servings|16   Time|3 hours 10 minutes

Nutritional Content (per serving):

Cal| 164   Fat| 0.3g   Protein| 4.3g   Carbs| 32.6g   Fibre| 1.4g

Ingredients:

- Water (360 millilitres, warm)
- White sugar (25 grams)
- Bread flour (610 grams)
- Caraway seeds (20 grams)
- Raisins (95 grams)
- Margarine (30 grams)
- Salt (5 grams)
- Dry milk powder (30 grams)
- Active dry yeast (6 grams)

Directions:

1. Place all ingredients except for raisins in the baking pan of bread machine in the order recommended by manufacturer.
2. Place the baking pan in bread machine and close with lid.
3. Select "Fruit Bread" setting.
4. Press start button.
5. Wait for bread machine to beep before adding the raisins.
6. Carefully remove the baking pan from machine and then invert the bread loaf onto a wire rack to cool completely before slicing.
7. Cut the bread loaf into desired-sized slices and serve.

Sourdough Bread

Servings|14   Time|3¾ hours
Nutritional Content (per serving):
Cal| 207   Fat| 0.6g   Protein| 5.8g   Carbs| 43.7g   Fibre| 1.6g

Ingredients:

For Starter:

- Water (960 millilitres lukewarm)
- Bread machine yeast (4½ grams)
- Bread flour (405 grams)
- White sugar (40 grams)

For Bread:

- Water (120 millilitres)
- Bread flour (405 grams)
- White sugar (25 grams)
- Salt (7½ grams)
- Bread machine yeast (3 grams)

Directions:

1. For starter: place water and yeast in the bowl of stand mixer and mix until dissolved completely. Let it rest for 2-3 minutes.
2. Add flour and sugar and beat on medium speed until a smooth dough forms.
3. Transfer the dough into a glass bowl.
4. With a kitchen wrap, cover the bowl loosely and set aside at room temperature for 1 week, stirring after every 12 hours.
5. On last day, stir the starter well.
6. Place about 225-230 grams of starter and all the bread ingredients in the baking pan of bread machine in the order recommended by manufacturer.
7. Place the baking pan in bread machine and close with lid.
8. Select "Basic" setting and then "Light Crust".
9. Press start button.
10. Carefully remove the baking pan from machine and then invert the bread loaf onto a wire rack to cool completely before slicing.
11. Cut the bread loaf into desired-sized slices and serve.

Challah Bread

Servings|16   Time|3 hours 20 minutes
Nutritional Content (per serving):
Cal| 229   Fat| 7.5g   Protein| 5.4g   Carbs| 34.7g   Fibre| 5.4g

Ingredients:

- Water (360 millilitres)
- Salt (5 grams)
- Bread flour (610 grams)
- Active dry yeast (9 grams)
- 5 large egg yolks
- (90 millilitres) Canola oil
- (85 grams) brown sugar
- Large egg (1, lightly beaten)

Directions:

1. Place all ingredients except for egg in the baking pan of bread machine in the order recommended by manufacturer.
2. Place the baking pan in bread machine and close with lid.
3. Select "Dough" cycle.
4. Press start button.
5. After "Dough" cycle completes, remove the dough from bread pan and place onto a lightly floured surface.
6. Divide the dough in 2 portions and then, cut each into three sections.
7. Now, roll each section into a long strand.
8. With your fingers, pinch the ends of three strands together firmly and braid from middle.
9. Repeat with remaining dough portion.
10. Arrange the braids onto a large greased baking sheet.
11. With a plastic wrap, cover the baking sheet and set aside in a warm place for 30 minutes or until doubled in size.
12. Preheat your oven to 350°F.
13. Uncover the baking sheet and brush the braids with beaten egg.
14. Bake for approximately 30 minutes or until golden brown.
15. Remove the bread pan from oven and place onto a wire rack to cool for about 10 minutes.
16. Now, invert the bread onto the wire rack to cool completely before slicing.
17. Cut the bread into desired-sized slices and serve.

Millet & Cornmeal Bread

Servings|12   Time|1 hour 35 minutes

Nutritional Content (per serving):

Cal| 228   Fat| 4.8g   Protein| 5.6g   Carbs| 4.5g   Fibre| 3.6g

Ingredients:

- Water (310 millilitres)
- Honey (90 grams)
- Whole-wheat flour (195 grams)
- Yellow cornmeal (70 grams)
- Active dry yeast (7½ grams)
- Canola oil (45 millilitres)
- Bread flour (205 grams)
- Millet (90 grams)
- Salt (10 grams)

Directions:

1. Place all ingredients in the baking pan of bread machine in the order recommended by manufacturer.
2. Place the baking pan in bread machine and close with lid.
3. Select "Basic" setting.
4. Press start button.
5. Carefully remove the baking pan from machine and then invert the bread loaf onto a wire rack to cool completely before slicing.
6. Cut the bread loaf into desired-sized slices and serve.

Rice Flour Bread

Servings|12   Time|4 hours 35 minutes

Nutritional Content (per serving):

Cal| 20   Fat| 4.6g   Protein| 6.9g   Carbs| 36.4g   Fibre| 2.1g

Ingredients:

- Large eggs (3, beaten)
- Vegetable oil (45 millilitres)
- White rice flour (405 grams)
- Dry milk powder (115 grams)
- Xanthan gum (15 grams)
- Salt (7½ grams)
- Water (360 millilitres, warm)
- Apple cider vinegar (5 millilitres)
- White sugar (40 grams)
- Active dry yeast (6¾ grams)

Directions:

1. In
2. Place eggs, water, oil and vinegar in a bowl and beat well.
3. In a separate bowl, place rice flour, Whole milk powder, sugar, xanthan gum, yeast and salt and mix well.
4. Place the egg mixture in the baking pan of bread machine and top with flour mixture.
5. Place the baking pan in bread machine and close with lid.
6. Select "Whole Wheat" setting and then "Medium Crust".
7. Press start button.
8. Carefully remove the baking pan from machine and then invert the bread loaf onto a wire rack to cool completely before slicing.
9. Cut the bread loaf into desired-sized slices and serve.

Multi-Grain Cereal Bread

Servings|12 Time|3 hours 35 minutes

Nutritional Content (per serving):

Cal| 150   Fat| 2.8g   Protein| 4.3g   Carbs| 27.1g   Fibre| 2.6g

Ingredients:

- Water (300 millilitres)
- Bread flour (180 grams)
- Whole-wheat flour (180 grams)
- Brown sugar (30 grams)
- Bread machine yeast (7½ grams)
- 1 Margarine (30 grams, softened)
- Uncooked multi-grain cereal (30 grams)
- Salt (5 grams)

Directions:

1. Place all ingredients in the baking pan of bread machine in the order recommended by manufacturer.
2. Place the baking pan in bread machine and close with lid.
3. Select "Basic" setting and then "Medium Crust".
4. Press start button.
5. Carefully remove the baking pan from machine and then invert the bread loaf onto a wire rack to cool completely before slicing.
6. Cut the bread loaf into desired-sized slices and serve.

Mixed Seeds Bread

Servings|12   Time|3 hours 5 minutes

Nutritional Content (per serving):

Cal| 185   Fat| 7.3g   Protein| 5.5g   Carbs| 25g   Fibre| 2.9g

Ingredients:

- Water (240 millilitres, lukewarm)
- Mixed seeds (sunflower, pumpkin, poppy, sesame) (60 grams)
- Olive oil (60 millilitres)
- White flour (260 grams)
- Whole-wheat flour (130 grams)
- Salt (5 grams)
- Dry yeast (4½ grams)

Directions:

1. Place all ingredients in the baking pan of bread machine in the order recommended by manufacturer.
2. Place the baking pan in bread machine and close with lid.
3. Select "White Bread" setting.
4. Press start button.
5. Carefully remove the baking pan from machine and then invert the bread loaf onto a wire rack to cool completely before slicing.
6. Cut the bread loaf into desired-sized slices and serve.

Date & Almond Bread

Servings|16   Time|2 hours 5 minutes

Nutritional Content (per serving):

Cal| 103   Fat| 3.4g   Protein| 2g   Carbs| 16.7g   Fibre| 1.2g

Ingredients:

- Dates (110 grams, pitted and chopped)
- Water (180 millilitres boiling)
- All-purpose flour (195 grams)
- Baking powder (4 grams)
- Vanilla extract (5 millilitres)
- Unsalted butter (40 grams, cut into ½-inch pieces)
- White sugar (25 grams)
- Baking soda (4 grams)
- Salt (2½ grams)
- Almonds (40 grams, chopped)

Directions:

1. Place all ingredients in the baking pan of bread machine in the order recommended by manufacturer.
2. Place the baking pan in bread machine and close with lid.
3. Select "Quick Bread" setting and then "Medium Crust".
4. Press start button.
5. After the mixing of mixture for 4 minutes, stir sides and bottom with rubber scraper for complete mixing.
6. Carefully remove the baking pan from machine and then invert the bread loaf onto a wire rack to cool completely before slicing.
7. Cut the bread loaf into desired-sized slices and serve.

Walnut Bread

Servings|8   Time|3 hours 10 minutes

Nutritional Content (per serving):

Cal| 192   Fat| 5.6g   Protein| 6.3g   Carbs| 29.4g   Fibre| 1.4g

Ingredients:

- Water (160 millilitres)
- Unsalted butter (15 grams, chopped)
- Salt (2½ grams)
- Walnuts (50 grams, toasted and chopped roughly)
- Large egg white (1)
- Dry milk powder (15 grams)
- White sugar (15 grams)
- Bread flour (270 grams)
- Bread machine yeast (3 grams)

Directions:

1. Place all ingredients in the baking pan of bread machine in the order recommended by the manufacturer, adding walnuts with flour.
2. Place the baking pan in bread machine and close with lid.
3. Select "Basic" setting and then "Medium Crust".
4. Press start button.
5. Carefully remove the baking pan from machine and then invert the bread loaf onto a wire rack to cool completely before slicing.
6. Cut the bread loaf into desired-sized slices and serve.

Mango Bread

Servings|10   Time|3 hours 5 minutes

Nutritional Content (per serving):

Cal| 147   Fat| 0.9g   Protein| 3.8g   Carbs| 31.1g   Fibre| 1.1g

Ingredients:

- Fresh mango nectar (185 millilitres)
- Honey (60 grams)
- Bread flour (270 grams)
- Dried mango (170 grams, chopped very finely)
- Large egg (1, beaten)
- Unsalted butter (30 grams, melted and cooled)
- Salt (5 grams)
- Dry milk powder (30 grams)
- Quick-rising yeast (6 grams)

Directions:

1. Place all ingredients except dried mango in the baking pan of bread machine in the order recommended by manufacturer.
2. Place the baking pan in bread machine and close with lid.
3. Select "Sweet Bread" setting.
4. Press start button.
5. Wait for bread machine to beep before adding mango.
6. Carefully remove the baking pan from machine and then invert the bread loaf onto a wire rack to cool completely before slicing.
7. Cut the bread loaf into desired-sized slices and serve.

Banana Oat Bread

Servings|12   Time|3 hours 5 minutes

Nutritional Content (per serving):

Cal| 260   Fat| 4.3g   Protein| 6.5g   Carbs| 50.1g   Fibre| 4.4g

Ingredients:

- Water (120 millilitres)
- Bananas (5, peeled and mashed)
- All-purpose flour (325 grams)
- Active dry yeast (6 grams)
- Olive oil (30 millilitres)
- Honey (40 grams)
- Rolled oats (270 grams)
- Salt (5 grams)

Directions:

1. Place all ingredients in the baking pan of bread machine in the order recommended by manufacturer.
2. Place the baking pan in bread machine and close with lid.
3. Select "Sweet Bread" setting.
4. Press start button.
5. Carefully remove the baking pan from machine and then invert the bread loaf onto a wire rack to cool completely before slicing.
6. Cut the bread loaf into desired-sized slices and serve.

Apple Bread

Servings|12   Time|3 hours 40 minutes

Nutritional Content (per serving):

Cal| 187   Fat| 5.1g   Protein| 4.1g   Carbs| 31.5g   Fibre| 1.8g

Ingredients:

- Water (240 millilitres)
- Bread flour (405 grams)
- Brown sugar (40 grams)
- Ground cinnamon (2½ grams)
- Apple (60 grams, cored and chopped)
- Unsalted butter (30 grams, softened)
- Brown sugar (40 grams)
- Salt (5 grams)
- Pecans (45 grams, toasted and chopped roughly)

Directions:

1. Place all ingredients except for apple and pecans in the baking pan of bread machine in the order recommended by manufacturer.
2. Place the baking pan in bread machine and close with lid.
3. Select "Basic" setting and then "Light Crust".
4. Press start button.
5. Wait for bread machine to beep before adding apple and pecans.
6. Carefully remove the baking pan from machine and then invert the bread loaf onto a wire rack to cool completely before slicing.
7. Cut the bread loaf into desired-sized slices and serve.

Blueberry Bread

Servings|12   Time|3 hours 10 minutes

Nutritional Content (per serving):

Cal| 224   Fat| 4g   Protein| 6g   Carbs| 40.7g   Fibre| 1.5g

Ingredients:

- Whole milk (240 millilitres)
- Water (60 millilitres)
- Bread flour (540 grams)
- White sugar (50 grams)
- Ground nutmeg (2½ grams)
- Dried blueberries (75 grams)
- Large egg (1, beaten)
- Unsalted butter (40 grams, chopped)
- Salt (5 grams)
- Active dry yeast (3¾ grams)

Directions:

1. Place all ingredients except for blueberries in the baking pan of bread machine in the order recommended by manufacturer.
2. Place the baking pan in bread machine and close with lid.
3. Select "Basic" setting and then "Medium Crust".
4. Press start button.
5. Wait for bread machine to beep before adding blueberries.
6. Carefully remove the baking pan from machine and then invert the bread loaf onto a wire rack to cool completely before slicing.
7. Cut the bread loaf into desired-sized slices and serve.

Lemon Bread

Servings|16   Time|3 hours 10 minutes

Nutritional Content (per serving):

Cal| 133   Fat| 3.2g   Protein| 3.4g   Carbs| 22.5g   Fibre| 1g

Ingredients:

- Water (150 millilitres)
- Fresh lemon juice (45 millilitres)
- Poppy seeds (20 grams)
- Salt (5 grams)
- Bread flour (405 grams)
- Large egg (1, beaten)
- Unsalted butter (40 grams)
- White sugar (40 grams)
- Lemon rind (10 grams, grated)
- Ground nutmeg (2¼ grams)
- Bread machine yeast (6 grams)

Directions:

1. Place all ingredients in the baking pan of bread machine in the order recommended by manufacturer.
2. Place the baking pan in bread machine and close with lid.
3. Select "Basic" setting and then "Medium Crust".
4. Press start button.
5. Carefully remove the baking pan from machine and then invert the bread loaf onto a wire rack to cool completely before slicing.
6. Cut the bread loaf into desired-sized slices and serve.

Carrot Bread

Servings|16   Time|3 hours 10 minutes

Nutritional Content (per serving):

Cal| 140   Fat| 1.9g   Protein| 4.7g   Carbs| 25.6g   Fibre| 1.5g

Ingredients:

- Water (205-210 millilitres)
- Canola oil (20 millilitres)
- Bread flour (270 grams)
- Whole-wheat flour (85 grams)
- Brown sugar (20 grams)
- Active dry yeast (4½ grams)
- Dry milk powder (60 grams)
- Carrot (60 grams, peeled and grated)
- Rolled oats (120 grams)
- Salt (5 grams)

Directions:

1. Place all ingredients in the baking pan of bread machine in the order recommended by manufacturer.
2. Place the baking pan in bread machine and close with lid.
3. Select "Sweet Bread" setting.
4. Press start button.
5. Carefully remove the baking pan from machine and then invert the bread loaf onto a wire rack to cool completely before slicing.
6. Cut the bread loaf into desired-sized slices and serve.

Courgette Raisin Bread

Servings|12   Time|2 hours 10 minutes

Nutritional Content (per serving):

Cal| 187   Fat| 8.9g   Protein| 3.4g   Carbs| 24.3g   Fibre| 1g

Ingredients:

- Vegetable oil (90 millilitres)
- Large eggs (2, beaten)
- White sugar (40 grams)
- Ground cinnamon (5 grams)
- Baking powder (2 grams)
- Walnuts (20 grams, chopped)
- Courgette (70 grams, shredded)
- Brown sugar (60 grams)
- All-purpose flour (195 grams)
- Salt (5 grams)
- Baking soda (2 grams)
- Raisins (55 grams)

Directions:

1. Place all ingredients in the baking pan of bread machine in the order recommended by manufacturer.
2. Place the baking pan in bread machine and close with lid.
3. Select "Quick Bread" setting.
4. Press start button.
5. Carefully remove the baking pan from machine and then invert the bread loaf onto a wire rack to cool completely before slicing.
6. Cut the bread loaf into desired-sized slices and serve.

Two Sugars Bread

Servings|12   Time|3 hours

Nutritional Content (per serving):

Cal| 204   Fat| 4.9g   Protein| 4.9g   Carbs| 35.4g   Fibre| 1.7g

Ingredients:

- Whole milk (240 millilitres)
- Large egg (1, beaten)
- Brown sugar (40 grams)
- Ground cinnamon (15 grams)
- Bread flour (405 grams)
- Unsalted butter (55 grams, softened)
- White sugar (50 grams)
- Salt (1¼ grams)
- Bread machine yeast (6 grams)

Directions:

1. Place all ingredients in the baking pan of bread machine in the order recommended by manufacturer.
2. Place the baking pan in bread machine and close with lid.
3. Select "Sweet Bread" setting and then "Medium Crust".
4. Press start button.
5. Carefully remove the baking pan from machine and then invert the bread loaf onto a wire rack to cool completely before slicing.
6. Cut the bread loaf into desired-sized slices and serve.

Molasses Whole-Wheat Bread

Servings|12   Time|4 hours 5 minutes

Nutritional Content (per serving):

Cal| 207   Fat| 3.7g   Protein| 5.6g   Carbs| 38.3g   Fibre| 2.9g

Ingredients:

- Whole milk (90 millilitres)
- Molasses (60 grams)
- Bread flour (270 grams)
- Whole-wheat flour (230 grams)
- Salt (5 grams)
- Water (60 millilitres)
- Unsalted butter (40 grams, softened)
- White sugar (30 grams)
- Quick-rising yeast (7 grams)

Directions:

1. Place all ingredients in the baking pan of bread machine in the order recommended by manufacturer.
2. Place the baking pan in bread machine and close with lid.
3. Select "Light Browning" setting.
4. Press start button.
5. Carefully remove the baking pan from machine and then invert the bread loaf onto a wire rack to cool completely before slicing.
6. Cut the bread loaf into desired-sized slices and serve.

Honey Bread

Servings|16   Time|2 hours 5 minutes

Nutritional Content (per serving):

Cal| 131   Fat| 2.6g   Protein| 3.3g   Carbs| 23.4g   Fibre| 0.8g

Ingredients:

- Whole milk (255 millilitres)
- Unsalted butter (40 grams, melted)
- Active dry yeast (6 grams)
- Honey (60 grams)
- Bread flour (405 grams)
- Salt (7½ grams)

Directions:

1. Place all ingredients in the baking pan of bread machine in the order recommended by manufacturer.
2. Place the baking pan in bread machine and close with lid.
3. Select "White Bread" setting and then "Medium Crust".
4. Press start button.
5. Carefully remove the baking pan from machine and then invert the bread loaf onto a wire rack to cool completely before slicing.
6. Cut the bread loaf into desired-sized slices and serve.

Maple Bread

Servings|12   Time|3 hours 5 minutes

Nutritional Content (per serving):

Cal| 166   Fat| 2.6g   Protein| 5.7g   Carbs| 28.9g   Fibre| 0.4g

Ingredients:

- Buttermilk (240 millilitres)
- Vegetable oil (30 millilitres)
- Whole-wheat flour (130 grams)
- Bread machine yeast (4½ grams)
- Maple syrup (40 grams)
- Dry milk powder (30 grams)
- Bread flour (270 grams)
- Salt (5 grams)

Directions:

1. Place all ingredients in the baking pan of bread machine in the order recommended by manufacturer.
2. Place the baking pan in bread machine and close with lid.
3. Select "Basic" setting.
4. Press start button.
5. Carefully remove the baking pan from machine and then invert the bread loaf onto a wire rack to cool completely before slicing.
6. Cut the bread loaf into desired-sized slices and serve.

Peanut Butter Jelly Bread

Servings|12   Time|3 hours 5 minutes

Nutritional Content (per serving):

Cal| 236   Fat| 7.3g   Protein| 6.8g   Carbs| 35.9g   Fibre| 1.1g

Ingredients:

- Water (240 millilitres)
- Peanut butter (125 grams)
- White sugar (15 grams)
- Whole-wheat flour (130 grams)
- Active dry yeast (4½ grams)
- Vegetable oil (25 millilitres)
- Blackberry jelly (115 grams)
- Salt (5 grams)
- Bread flour (270 grams)

Directions:

1. Place all ingredients in the baking pan of bread machine in the order recommended by manufacturer.
2. Place the baking pan in bread machine and close with lid.
3. Select "Sweet Bread" setting.
4. Press start button.
5. Carefully remove the baking pan from machine and then invert the bread loaf onto a wire rack to cool completely before slicing.
6. Cut the bread loaf into desired-sized slices and serve.

Raisin Bread

Servings|12   Time|3 hours 5 minutes

Nutritional Content (per serving):

Cal| 184   Fat| 2.4g   Protein| 4.1g   Carbs| 36.9g   Fibre| 1.6g

Ingredients:

- Water (240 millilitres)
- Bread flour (405 grams)
- Salt (5 grams)
- Active dry yeast (7½ grams)
- Margarine (30 grams)
- White sugar (40 grams)
- Ground cinnamon (5 grams)
- Raisins (10 grams)

Directions:

1. Place all ingredients except for raisins in the baking pan of bread machine in the order recommended by manufacturer.
2. Place the baking pan in bread machine and close with lid.
3. Select "Sweet Bread" setting.
4. Press start button.
5. Wait for bread machine to beep before adding raisins.
6. Carefully remove the baking pan from machine and then invert the bread loaf onto a wire rack to cool completely before slicing.
7. Cut the bread loaf into desired-sized slices and serve.

Currant Bread

Servings|10   Time|3 hours 40 minutes

Nutritional Content (per serving):

Cal| 244   Fat| 7g   Protein| 6.6g   Carbs| 39.2g   Fibre| 2g

Ingredients:

- Whole milk (300 millilitres, warm)
- Bread flour (405 grams)
- Salt (5 grams)
- Cashews (65 grams, chopped finely)
- Olive oil (30 millilitres)
- Maple syrup (40 grams)
- Ground cardamom (10 grams)
- Active dry yeast (6 grams)
- Currants (75 grams)

Directions:

1. Place all ingredients except for currants and cashews in the baking pan of bread machine in the order recommended by manufacturer.
2. Place the baking pan in bread machine and close with lid.
3. Select "Basic" setting.
4. Press start button.
5. Wait for bread machine to beep before adding currants and cashews.
6. Carefully remove the baking pan from machine and then invert the bread loaf onto a wire rack to cool completely before slicing.
7. Cut the bread loaf into desired-sized slices and serve.

Pineapple Bread

Servings|12 Time|3 hours 5 minutes

Nutritional Content (per serving):

Cal| 180   Fat| 3g   Protein| 5.1g   Carbs| 32.7g   Fibre| 1.1g

Ingredients:

- Fresh pineapple juice (180 millilitres)
- Honey (50 grams)
- Bread flour (405 grams)
- Quick-rising yeast (6 grams)
- Large egg (1)
- Vegetable oil (30 millilitres)
- Salt (2½ grams)
- Dry milk powder (30 grams)

Directions:

1. Place all ingredients in the baking pan of bread machine in the order recommended by manufacturer.
2. Place the baking pan in bread machine and close with lid.
3. Select "Sweet Bread" setting and then "Light Crust".
4. Press start button.
5. Carefully remove the baking pan from machine and then invert the bread loaf onto a wire rack to cool completely before slicing.
6. Cut the bread loaf into desired-sized slices and serve.

Pumpkin Bread

Servings|14   Time|1 hour 5 minutes

Nutritional Content (per serving):

Cal| 157   Fat| 3.5g   Protein| 4.6g   Carbs| 26.7g   Fibre| 1.3g

Ingredients:

- Warm water (150 millilitres)
- Unsalted butter (55 grams, softened)
- Bread flour (370 grams)
- Salt (2½ grams)
- Ground ginger (2½ grams)
- 1 Canned pumpkin puree (115 grams)
- Dry milk powder (60 grams)
- Brown sugar (45 grams)
- Ground cinnamon (5 grams)
- Active dry yeast (7 grams)

Directions:

1. Place all ingredients in the baking pan of bread machine in the order recommended by manufacturer.
2. Place the baking pan in bread machine and close with lid.
3. Select "Basic" setting.
4. Press start button.
5. Carefully remove the baking pan from machine and then invert the bread loaf onto a wire rack to cool completely before slicing.
6. Cut the bread loaf into desired-sized slices and serve.

Pumpkin Cranberry Bread

Servings|12   Time|4 hours 10 minutes

Nutritional Content (per serving):

Cal| 200   Fat| 5.3g   Protein| 5.1g   Carbs| 33.2g   Fibre| 3g

Ingredients:

- Water (180 millilitres)
- Brown sugar (30 grams)
- All-purpose flour (260 grams)
- Salt (5 grams)
- Walnuts (50 grams, chopped)
- Active dry yeast (5¼ grams)
- Canned pumpkin (65 grams)
- Vegetable oil (30 millilitres)
- Whole-wheat flour (130 grams)
- Sweetened dried cranberries (65 grams)

Directions:

1. Place all ingredients in the baking pan of bread machine in the order recommended by manufacturer.
2. Place the baking pan in bread machine and close with lid.
3. Select "Basic" setting.
4. Press start button.
5. Carefully remove the baking pan from machine and then invert the bread loaf onto a wire rack to cool completely before slicing.
6. Cut the bread loaf into desired-sized slices and serve.

Banana Pecans Bread

Servings|10   Time|1¼ hours

Nutritional Content (per serving):

Cal| 358   Fat| 16.4g   Protein| 5.4g   Carbs| 49.9g   Fibre| 2.3g

Ingredients:

- Whole milk (90 millilitres)
- Unsalted butter (115 grams, melted)
- Sour cream (65 grams)
- White sugar (200 grams)
- Salt (2½ grams)
- Baking soda (4 grams)
- Medium eggs (2, beaten)
- Vanilla extract (5 millilitres)
- Medium, very ripe bananas (3, peeled and mashed)
- All-purpose flour (260 grams)
- Baking powder (6 grams)
- Pecans (60 grams, chopped)

Directions:

1. Place all ingredients in the baking pan of bread machine in the order recommended by manufacturer.
2. Place the baking pan in bread machine and close with lid.
3. Select "Quick Bread" setting and then "Medium Crust".
4. Press start button.
5. Carefully remove the baking pan from machine and then invert the bread loaf onto a wire rack to cool completely before slicing.
6. Cut the bread loaf into desired-sized slices and serve.

Cranberry Bread

Servings|16   Time|3 hours 10 minutes

Nutritional Content (per serving):

Cal| 156   Fat| 1.9g   Protein| 3.7g   Carbs| 30.6g   Fibre| 1.2g

Ingredients:

- Water (285 millilitres)
- Unsalted butter (30 grams, softened)
- Bread machine yeast (6 grams)
- Honey (80 grams)
- Bread flour (540 grams)
- Salt (5 grams)
- Dried cranberries (100 grams)

Directions:

1. Place all ingredients except the cranberries in the baking pan of bread machine in the order recommended by manufacturer.
2. Place the baking pan in bread machine and close with lid.
3. Select "Sweet Bread" setting.
4. Press start button.
5. Wait for bread machine to beep before adding cranberries.
6. Carefully remove the baking pan from machine and then invert the bread loaf onto a wire rack to cool completely before slicing.
7. Cut the bread loaf into desired-sized slices and serve.

Cranberry Orange Bread

Servings|12   Time|3 hours 10 minutes

Nutritional Content (per serving):

Cal| 211   Fat| 7.4g   Protein| 4.5g   Carbs| 31.2g   Fibre| 1.4g

Ingredients:

- All-purpose flour (390 grams)
- Plain yoghurt (185 grams)
- Honey (60 grams)
- Active dry yeast (6 grams)
- Salt (7½ grams)
- Dried cranberries (130 grams)
- Water (120 millilitres, warm)
- Unsalted butter (15 grams, melted)
- Orange oil (5 millilitres)

Directions:

1. Place all ingredients in the baking pan of bread machine in the order recommended by manufacturer.
2. Place the baking pan in bread machine and close with lid.
3. Select "Basic" setting and then "Light Crust".
4. Press start button.
5. Carefully remove the baking pan from machine and then invert the bread loaf onto a wire rack to cool completely before slicing.
6. Cut the bread loaf into desired-sized slices and serve.

Raspberry Bread

Servings|10   Time|2 hours 25 minutes

Nutritional Content (per serving):

Cal| 179   Fat| 5.1g   Protein| 5.5g   Carbs| 28.1g   Fibre| 4.1g

Ingredients:

- 1 Water (180 millilitres, hot)
- Chardonnay wine (60 millilitres)
- Frozen unsweetened raspberries (60 grams)
- Bread flour (70 grams)
- All-purpose flour (130 grams)
- Active dry yeast (7 grams)
- Caraway seeds (2½ grams)
- White sugar (50 grams)
- Chai tea powder (30 grams)
- Vanilla extract (2½ millilitres)
- Large egg yolk (1)
- Unsalted butter (15 grams, softened)
- Rye flour (30 grams)
- Wheat bran (30 grams)
- Walnuts (50 grams, chopped roughly)

Directions:

1. In a heatproof bowl, add hot water and chai tea package and stir to combine.
2. Set aside to cool for about 10 minutes.
3. Place chai tea and remaining ingredients in the baking pan of bread machine in the order recommended by manufacturer.
4. Place the baking pan in bread machine and close with lid.
5. Select "Sweet" setting and then "Light Crust".
6. Press start button.
7. Carefully remove the baking pan from machine and then invert the bread onto a wire rack to cool completely before serving.
8. Cut the bread loaf into desired-sized slices and serve.

Orange Honey Bread

Servings|12   Time|3 hours 10 minutes

Nutritional Content (per serving):

Cal| 192   Fat| 2.5g   Protein| 6.2g   Carbs| 36.4g   Fibre| 2.3g

Ingredients:

- Water (300 millilitres)
- Vegetable oil (20 millilitres)
- Bread flour (340 grams)
- Whole-wheat flour (50 grams)
- Active dry yeast (7 grams)
- Dry milk powder (45 grams)
- Honey (60 grams)
- Amaranth flour (90 grams)
- Orange zest (25 grams, grated finely)

Directions:

1. Place all ingredients in the baking pan of bread machine in the order recommended by manufacturer.
2. Place the baking pan in bread machine and close with lid.
3. Select "Basic" setting.
4. Press start button.
5. Carefully remove the baking pan from machine and then invert the bread loaf onto a wire rack to cool completely before slicing.
6. Cut the bread loaf into desired-sized slices and serve.

Banana Chocolate Bread

Servings|16   Time|1 hour 50 minutes

Nutritional Content (per serving):

Cal| 217   Fat| 8.3g   Protein| 3.3g   Carbs| 33.6g   Fibre| 1.2g

Ingredients:

- Whole milk (120 millilitres, warm)
- Vanilla extract (5 millilitres)
- Medium ripe bananas (3, peeled and mashed)
- Salt (2½ grams)
- Mini chocolate chips (80 grams)
- Large eggs (2)
- Unsalted butter (115 grams, melted)
- White sugar (200 grams)
- All-purpose flour (260 grams)
- Baking powder (8 grams)
- Baking soda (4 grams)

Directions:

1. Place all ingredients except for cranberries in the baking pan of bread machine in the order recommended by manufacturer.
2. Place the baking pan in bread machine and close with lid.
3. Select "Quick Bread" setting.
4. Press start button.
5. Wait for bread machine to beep before adding chocolate chips.
6. Carefully remove the baking pan from machine and then invert the bread loaf onto a wire rack to cool completely before slicing.
7. Cut the bread loaf into desired-sized slices and serve.

Sweet Potato Bread

Servings|16   Time|3 hours 10 minutes

Nutritional Content (per serving):

Cal| 169   Fat| 1.9g   Protein| 4.5g   Carbs| 32.9g   Fibre| 1.4g

Ingredients:

- Water (120 millilitres, warm)
- Sweet potato (150 grams, boiled, peeled and mashed)
- Unsalted butter (30 grams, softened)
- Active dry yeast (6 grams)
- Vanilla extract (5 millilitres)
- Bread flour (540 grams)
- Ground cinnamon (2½ grams)
- Brown sugar (65 grams)
- Salt (5 grams)
- Dry milk powder (30 grams)

Directions:

1. Place all ingredients in the baking pan of bread machine in the order recommended by manufacturer.
2. Place the baking pan in bread machine and close with lid.
3. Select "White Bread" setting.
4. Press start button.
5. Carefully remove the baking pan from machine and then invert the bread loaf onto a wire rack to cool completely before slicing.
6. Cut the bread loaf into desired-sized slices and serve.

Gingerbread

Servings|12   Time|3 hours 10 minutes

Nutritional Content (per serving):

Cal| 214   Fat| 3.8g   Protein| 5.3g   Carbs| 39.7g   Fibre| 1.5g

Ingredients:

- Whole milk (180 millilitres)
- Large egg (1)
- Bread flour (455 grams)
- Salt (5 grams)
- Ground ginger (2½ grams)
- Raisins (55 grams)
- Molasses (80 grams)
- Unsalted butter (40 grams)
- Brown sugar (10 grams)
- Ground cinnamon (2½ grams)
- Active dry yeast (7 grams)

Directions:

1. Place all ingredients except for raisins in the baking pan of bread machine in the order recommended by manufacturer.
2. Place the baking pan in bread machine and close with lid.
3. Select "Basic" setting and then "Light Crust".
4. Press start button.
5. Wait for bread machine to beep before adding raisins.
6. Carefully remove the baking pan from machine and then invert the bread loaf onto a wire rack to cool completely before slicing.
7. Cut the bread loaf into desired-sized slices and serve.

Mustard Bread

Servings|12   Time|3 hours 5 minutes

Nutritional Content (per serving):

Cal| 163   Fat| 3.4g   Protein| 5.5g   Carbs| 28.4g   Fibre| 3.2g

Ingredients:

- Water (240 millilitres, warm)
- Olive oil (30 millilitres)
- All-purpose flour (260 grams)
- Whole-wheat flour (85 grams)
- Active dry yeast (7½ grams)
- Dijon mustard (130 grams)
- Molasses (25 grams)
- Rye flour (70 grams)
- Vital wheat gluten (11 grams)

Directions:

1. Place all ingredients in the baking pan of bread machine in the order recommended by manufacturer.
2. Place the baking pan in bread machine and close with lid.
3. Select "White Bread" setting.
4. Press start button.
5. Carefully remove the baking pan from machine and then invert the bread loaf onto a wire rack to cool completely before slicing.
6. Cut the bread loaf into desired-sized slices and serve.

Star Anise Bread

Servings|12   Time|3 hours 10 minutes

Nutritional Content (per serving):

Cal| 218   Fat| 5g   Protein| 5.2g   Carbs| 38.2g   Fibre| 2.5g

Ingredients:

- Whole milk (240 millilitres)
- Large egg (1, beaten)
- White sugar (75 grams)
- Bread flour (340 grams)
- Anise seeds (5 grams)
- Water (60 millilitres)
- Margarine (50 grams, softened)
- Yellow corn flour (150 grams)
- Salt (5 grams)
- Active dry yeast (7½ grams)

Directions:

1. Place all ingredients in the baking pan of bread machine in the order recommended by manufacturer.
2. Place the baking pan in bread machine and close with lid.
3. Select "White Bread" setting.
4. Press start button.
5. Carefully remove the baking pan from machine and then invert the bread loaf onto a wire rack to cool completely before slicing.
6. Cut the bread loaf into desired-sized slices and serve.

Orange Bread Cake

Servings|16   Time|1 hour 35 minutes

Nutritional Content (per serving):

Cal| 241   Fat| 3.9g   Protein| 5g   Carbs| 47.3g   Fibre| 0.8g

Ingredients:

- Fresh orange juice (240 millilitres)
- Medium eggs (3, slightly beaten)
- Cornstarch (100 grams)
- Baking powder (24 grams)
- Unsalted butter (55 grams, softened)
- White sugar (300 grams)
- Dry milk powder (60 grams)
- All-purpose flour (390 grams)

Directions:

1. Place all ingredients except for baking powder in the baking pan of bread machine in the order recommended by manufacturer.
2. Place the baking pan in bread machine and close with lid.
3. Select "Cake" setting and then "Medium Crust".
4. Press start button.
5. Wait for bread machine to beep before adding the baking powder.
6. Carefully remove the baking pan from machine and then invert the bread cake onto a wire rack to cool completely before glazing.
7. In a bowl, mix together confectioners' sugar and orange juice.
8. Spread the glaze over cake evenly.
9. Cut the bread cake into desired-sized slices and serve.

Chocolate Bread Cake

Servings|8   Time|1¼ hours

Nutritional Content (per serving):

Cal| 443   Fat| 17.2g   Protein| 7.4g   Carbs| 69.4g   Fibre| 2.6g

Ingredients:

- Whole milk (300 millilitres)
- Medium eggs (2)
- Self-rising flour (280 grams)
- Vanilla extract (5 millilitres)
- Unsalted butter (40 grams, softened)
- Cocoa powder (45 grams)
- White sugar (300 grams)

Directions:

1. Place all ingredients in the baking pan of bread machine in the order recommended by manufacturer.
2. Place the baking pan in bread machine and close with lid.
3. Select "Cake" setting and then "Medium Crust".
4. Press start button.
5. Carefully remove the baking pan from machine and then invert the bread cake onto a wire rack to cool completely before serving.
6. Cut the bread cake into desired-sized slices and serve.

Chocolate Chip Bread

Servings|12   Time|3 hours

Nutritional Content (per serving):

Cal| 214   Fat| 5.6g   Protein| 5.2g   Carbs| 35.7g   Fibre| 1.5g

Ingredients:

- Whole milk (240 millilitres)
- Large egg (1, beaten)
- Bread flour (405 grams)
- White sugar (30 grams)
- Semi-sweet mini chocolate chips (120 grams)
- Water (60 millilitres)
- Unsalted butter (30 grams, softened)
- Salt (5 grams)
- Active dry yeast (4½ grams)

Directions:

Place all ingredients except the chocolate chips in the baking pan of bread machine in the order recommended by manufacturer.

1. Place the baking pan in bread machine and close with lid.
2. Select "Mix Bread" setting.
3. Press start button.
4. Wait for bread machine to beep before adding chocolate chips.
5. Carefully remove the baking pan from machine and then invert the bread loaf onto a wire rack to cool completely before slicing.
6. Cut the bread loaf into desired-sized slices and serve.

Mocha Bread

Servings|12   Time|2¾ hours
Nutritional Content (per serving):
Cal| 170   Fat| 2.9g   Protein| 4.6g   Carbs| 30.8g   Fibre| 1.1g

Ingredients:

- Coffee-flavoured liqueur (30 millilitres)
- Salt (5 grams)
- Vegetable oil (10 millilitres)
- Semi-sweet mini chocolate chips (40 grams)
- Water (60 millilitres)
- Evaporated milk (1(150-millilitres) can)
- Bread flour (405 grams)
- Brown sugar (20 grams)
- Active dry yeast (3 grams)

Directions:

1. Place all ingredients except the chocolate chips in the baking pan of bread machine in the order recommended by manufacturer.
2. Place the baking pan in bread machine and close with lid.
3. Select "Dough" cycle.
4. Press start button.
5. After "Dough" cycle completes, remove the dough from bread pan and place onto lightly floured surface.
6. With a plastic wrap, cover the dough for about 10 minutes.
7. Uncover the dough and roll it into a rectangle.
8. Sprinkle the dough with chocolate chips and then shape into a loaf.
9. Now, place the dough into greased loaf pan.
10. With a plastic wrap, cover the loaf pan and place in a warm place for 45 minutes or doubled in size.
11. Preheat your oven to 375°F.
12. Bake for approximately 24-30 minutes or until a wooden skewer inserted in the center comes out clean.
13. Remove the loaf pan from oven and place onto a wire rack to cool for about 10 minutes.
14. Now, invert bread onto the wire rack to cool completely before slicing.
15. Cut the bread loaf into desired-sized slices and serve.

Sunflower Seed Oat Bread

Servings|14   Time|4 hours 5 minutes

Nutritional Content (per serving):

Cal| 244   Fat| 7.4g   Protein| 7.2g   Carbs| 38.4g   Fibre| 3.6g

Ingredients:

- Water (420 millilitres)
- Unsalted butter (30 grams, softened)
- Whole-wheat flour (260 grams)
- Dry milk powder (30 grams)
- Bread machine yeast (7½ grams)
- Honey (80 grams)
- Olive oil (30 millilitres)
- Bread flour (270 grams)
- Quick-cooking oats (60 grams)
- Salt (5 grams)
- Sunflower seeds (70 grams)

Directions:

1. Place all ingredients except for sunflower seeds in the baking pan of bread machine in the order recommended by manufacturer.
2. Place the baking pan in bread machine and close with lid.
3. Select "Basic" setting and then "Light Crust".
4. Press start button.
5. Wait for bread machine to beep before adding the sunflower seeds.
6. Carefully remove the baking pan from machine and then invert the bread loaf onto a wire rack to cool completely before slicing.
7. Cut the bread loaf into desired-sized slices and serve.

Ciabatta Bread

Servings|20   Time|1 hour 50 minutes
Nutritional Content (per serving):
Cal| 94   Fat| 1.7g   Protein| 2.4g   Carbs| 17.1g   Fibre| 2.4g

Ingredients:

- Water (360 millilitres)
- White sugar (5 grams)
- Bread machine yeast (4½ grams)
- Salt (7½ grams)
- Olive oil (30 millilitres)
- Bread flour (440 grams)

Directions:

1. Place all ingredients in the baking pan of bread machine in the order recommended by manufacturer.
2. Place the baking pan in bread machine and close with lid.
3. Select "Dough" cycle.
4. Press start button.
5. After "Dough" cycle completes, remove the dough from bread pan and place onto a generously floured surface.
6. With a greased plastic wrap, cover the dough for 15 minutes.
7. Line 2 baking sheets with parchment paper.
8. Divide the dough into 2 portions and then, shape each into a 3x14-inch oval.
9. Place 1 bread oval onto each prepared baking sheet and dust with flour lightly.
10. With a plastic wrap, cover each baking sheet and set aside in Warm for 45 minutes or until doubled in size.
11. Preheat your oven to 425°F.
12. Arrange the rack in the middle of oven.
13. Brush each loaf with water and bake for 25-30 minutes or until a wooden skewer inserted in the center comes out clean.
14. Remove the loaf pans from oven and place onto a wire rack to cool for about 10 minutes.
15. Now, invert each bread onto the wire rack to cool completely before serving.
16. Cut each bread loaf into desired-sized slices and serve.

Savory Bread Recipes

Mustard Curry Bread

Servings|10   Time|0 hours

Nutritional Content (per serving):

Cal| 184   Fat| 4g   Protein| 5.5g   Carbs| 32.2g   Fibre| 3.4g

Ingredients:

- Bread flour (230 grams)
- Dry milk powder (20 grams)
- Curry powder (15 grams)
- Water (300 millilitres)
- Olive oil (30 millilitres)
- Active dry yeast (9 grams)
- Whole-wheat flour (165 grams)
- Dry milk powder (20 grams)
- Salt (10 grams)
- Dijon mustard (45 grams)
- Honey (10 grams)

Directions:

1. Place all ingredients in the baking pan of bread machine in the order recommended by manufacturer.
2. Place the baking pan in bread machine and close with lid.
3. Select "Whole Wheat" setting.
4. Press start button.
5. Carefully remove the baking pan from machine and then invert the bread loaf onto a wire rack to cool completely before slicing.
6. Cut the bread loaf into desired-sized slices and serve.

Mustard Dill Bread

Servings|12   Time|3 hours 5 minutes

Nutritional Content (per serving):

Cal| 151   Fat| 1.7g   Protein| 5.5g   Carbs| 28.4g   Fibre| 2.1g

Ingredients:

- Water (240 millilitres)
- Unsalted butter (15 grams)
- Bread flour (270 grams)
- Dry milk powder (45 grams)
- Dill weed (5 grams)
- Dijon mustard (20 grams)
- Salt (5 grams)
- Whole-wheat flour (130 grams)
- Brown sugar (10 grams)
- Bread machine yeast (6 grams)

Directions:

1. Place all ingredients in the baking pan of bread machine in the order recommended by manufacturer.
2. Place the baking pan in bread machine and close with lid.
3. Select "Basic" setting and then "Medium Crust".
4. Press start button.
5. Carefully remove the baking pan from machine and then invert the bread loaf onto a wire rack to cool completely before slicing.
6. Cut the bread loaf into desired-sized slices and serve.

Tomato Rosemary Bread

Servings|12   Time|3 hours 40 minutes

Nutritional Content (per serving):

Cal| 123   Fat| 3.7g   Protein| 3.8g   Carbs| 18.7g   Fibre| 1g

Ingredients:

- Water (120 millilitres)
- Olive oil (30 millilitres)
- Salt (5 grams)
- Parmesan cheese (40 grams, grated)
- Sun-dried tomatoes (15 grams, chopped)
- Whole milk (60 millilitres)
- White sugar (5 grams)
- Fresh rosemary (5 grams, chopped)
- Bread flour (270 grams)
- Active dry yeast (6 grams)

Directions:

1. Place all ingredients except for tomato pieces in the baking pan of bread machine in the order recommended by manufacturer.
2. Place the baking pan in bread machine and close with lid.
3. Select "White Bread" setting.
4. Press start button.
5. Wait for bread machine to beep before adding the tomato pieces.
6. Carefully remove the baking pan from machine and then invert the bread loaf onto a wire rack to cool for at least 12-15 minutes before slicing.
7. Cut the bread loaf into desired-sized slices and serve warm.

Potato Bread

Servings|12   Time|3 hours 10 minutes

Nutritional Content (per serving):

Cal| 165   Fat| 3g   Protein| 4.4g   Carbs| 29.7g   Fibre| 1.2g

Ingredients:

- Whole milk (180 millilitres)
- Vegetable oil (30 millilitres)
- Bread flour (405 grams)
- White sugar (15 grams)
- Water (120 millilitres)
- Salt (5 grams)
- Instant potato flakes (25 grams)
- Ground white pepper (1¼ grams)
- Active dry yeast (6 grams)

Directions:

1. Place all ingredients in the baking pan of bread machine in the order recommended by manufacturer.
2. Place the baking pan in bread machine and close with lid.
3. Select "Basic" setting.
4. Press start button.
5. Carefully remove the baking pan from machine and then invert the bread loaf onto a wire rack to cool completely before slicing.
6. Cut the bread loaf into desired-sized slices and serve.

Parmesan Parsley Bread

Servings|12   Time|3¾ hours

Nutritional Content (per serving):

Cal| 205   Fat| 3.8g   Protein| 6.3g   Carbs| 36.1g   Fibre| 1.3g

Ingredients:

- Water (300 millilitres, hot)
- Fresh parsley (10 grams, chopped)
- White sugar (15 grams)
- Salt (5 grams)
- Bread flour yeast (3¾ grams)
- Olive oil (30 millilitres)
- Parmesan cheese (55 grams, shredded)
- Garlic cloves (2, minced)
- Bread flour (540 grams)

Directions:

1. Place all ingredients in the baking pan of bread machine in the order recommended by manufacturer.
2. Place the baking pan in bread machine and close with lid.
3. Select "Basic" setting.
4. Press start button.
5. Carefully remove the baking pan from machine and then invert the bread loaf onto a wire rack to cool completely before slicing.
6. Cut the bread loaf into desired-sized slices and serve.

Pepperoni Bread

Servings|12   Time|2¼ hours

Nutritional Content (per serving):

Cal| 200   Fat| 7.3g   Protein| 5.9g   Carbs| 27.7g   Fibre| 1.1g

Ingredients:

- Water (240 millilitres, warm)
- Bread flour (405 grams)
- Salt (5 grams)
- Dried onion (5 grams, minced)
- Mozzarella cheese (55 grams, shredded)
- Pepperoni slices (35 grams, chopped)
- Olive oil (60 millilitres)
- White sugar (15 grams)
- Garlic powder (5 grams)
- Dried basil (5 grams)
- Parmesan cheese (40 grams, grated)
- Bread machine yeast (6 grams)

Directions:

1. Place all ingredients in the baking pan of bread machine in the order recommended by manufacturer.
2. Place the baking pan in bread machine and close with lid.
3. Select "White Bread" setting.
4. Press start button.
5. Carefully remove the baking pan from machine and then invert the bread loaf onto a wire rack to cool completely before slicing.
6. Cut the bread loaf into desired-sized slices and serve.

Caramelized Onion Bread

Servings|12   Time|3 hours 40 minutes

Nutritional Content (per serving):

Cal| 157   Fat| 2.5g   Protein| 3.8g   Carbs| 29.7g   Fibre| 1.4g

Ingredients:

- ❖ Unsalted butter (15 grams)
- ❖ Water (240 millilitres)
- ❖ Bread flour (405 grams)
- ❖ Salt (5 grams)
- ❖ Medium onions (2, sliced)
- ❖ Vegetable oil (15 millilitres)
- ❖ White sugar (25 grams)
- ❖ Quick yeast 3¾ grams

Directions:

1. In a non-stick wok, melt butter over medium-low heat and cook onions for about 10-15 minutes, stirring occasionally.
2. Remove from the heat and set aside.
3. Place all ingredients except for cooked onion in the baking pan of bread machine in the order recommended by manufacturer.
4. Place the baking pan in bread machine and close with lid.
5. Select "Basic" setting.
6. Press start button.
7. Wait for bread machine to beep before adding the 25-30 grams of onions.
8. Carefully remove the baking pan from machine and then invert the bread loaf onto a wire rack to cool for at least 12-15 minutes before slicing.
9. Cut the bread loaf into desired-sized slices and serve warm.

Herbed Garlic Bread

Servings|12   Time|2 hours 10 minutes

Nutritional Content (per serving):

Cal| 142   Fat| 1.5g   Protein| 3.9g   Carbs| 28g   Fibre| 1.4g

Ingredients:

- Bread flour (405 grams)
- Unsalted butter (15 grams)
- Dry milk powder (15 grams)
- Active dry yeast (7 grams)
- Fresh thyme (5 grams, chopped)
- Water (300 millilitres, warm)
- White sugar (15 grams)
- Salt (5 grams)
- Fresh rosemary (5 grams, chopped)
- Garlic cloves (2, minced)

Directions:

1. Place all ingredients in the baking pan of bread machine in the order recommended by manufacturer.
2. Place the baking pan in bread machine and close with lid.
3. Select "White Bread" setting.
4. Press start button.
5. Carefully remove the baking pan from machine and then invert the bread loaf onto a wire rack to cool completely before slicing.
6. Cut the bread loaf into desired-sized slices and serve.

Cheddar Bread

Servings|12   Time|3 hours 10 minutes

Nutritional Content (per serving):

Cal| 187   Fat| 5g   Protein| 7.4g   Carbs| 27.4g   Fibre| 1g

Ingredients:

- Whole milk (240 millilitres, lukewarm)
- White sugar (15 grams)
- Better cheddar cheese powder (40 grams)
- Tabasco sauce (5 millilitres)
- All-purpose flour (390 grams)
- Salt (5 grams)
- Extra-sharp cheddar cheese (115 grams, grated)
- Instant yeast (4½ grams)

Directions:

1. Place all ingredients in the baking pan of bread machine in the order recommended by manufacturer.
2. Place the baking pan in bread machine and close with lid.
3. Select "Basic" setting and then "Light Crust".
4. Press start button.
5. Carefully remove the baking pan from machine and then invert the bread loaf onto a wire rack to cool completely before slicing.
6. Cut the bread loaf into desired-sized slices and serve.

Mixed Herbs Bread

Servings|8   Time|3 hours 10 minutes

Nutritional Content (per serving):

Cal| 221   Fat| 4.6g   Protein| 5.6g   Carbs| 39.1g   Fibre| 1.5g

Ingredients:

- Water (240 millilitres, warm)
- Salt (5 grams)
- Olive oil (30 millilitres)
- Dried oregano (5 grams)
- All-purpose flour (405 grams)
- Large egg (1, beaten)
- White sugar (25 grams)
- Dried rosemary (5 grams)
- Dried basil (5 grams)
- Bread machine yeast (6 grams)

Directions:

1. Place all ingredients in the baking pan of bread machine in the order recommended by manufacturer.
2. Place the baking pan in bread machine and close with lid.
3. Select "Basic" setting and then "Light Crust".
4. Press start button.
5. Carefully remove the baking pan from machine and then invert the bread loaf onto a wire rack to cool completely before slicing.
6. Cut the bread loaf into desired-sized slices and serve.

Chives Bread

Servings|10   Time|3 hours 10 minutes

Nutritional Content (per serving):

Cal| 183   Fat| 4.3 g   Protein| 5g   Carbs| 30.7g   Fibre| 1.2g

Ingredients:

- Whole milk (60 millilitres)
- Sour cream (60 grams)
- Bread flour (405 grams)
- Baking soda (½ grams)
- Salt (7½ grams)
- Active dry yeast (7 grams)
- Water (60 millilitres)
- Unsalted butter (30 grams, softened)
- White sugar (10 grams)
- Fresh chives (10 grams, minced)

Directions:

1. Place all ingredients in the baking pan of bread machine in the order recommended by manufacturer.
2. Place the baking pan in bread machine and close with lid.
3. Select "Basic" setting.
4. Press start button.
5. Carefully remove the baking pan from machine and then invert the bread loaf onto a wire rack to cool completely before slicing.
6. Cut the bread loaf into desired-sized slices and serve.

Rosemary Bread

Servings|12   Time|3 hours 10 minutes

Nutritional Content (per serving):

Cal| 139   Fat| 3.9g   Protein| 3.1g   Carbs| 22.9g   Fibre| 1.1g

Ingredients:

- Water (240 millilitres)
- White sugar (10 grams)
- Italian seasoning (1¼ grams)
- Dried rosemary (5 grams)
- Bread flour (340 grams)
- Olive oil (45 millilitres)
- Salt (7½ grams)
- Ground black pepper (1¼ grams)
- Active dry yeast (4½ grams)

Directions:

1. Place all ingredients in the baking pan of bread machine in the order recommended by manufacturer.
2. Place the baking pan in bread machine and close with lid.
3. Select "White Bread" setting.
4. Press start button.
5. Carefully remove the baking pan from machine and then invert the bread loaf onto a wire rack to cool completely before slicing.
6. Cut the bread loaf into desired-sized slices and serve.

Olives Bread

Servings|12   Time|2 hours 25 minutes

Nutritional Content (per serving):

Cal| 179   Fat| 6.3g   Protein| 3.9g   Carbs| 27.2g   Fibre| 1.9g

Ingredients:

- Water (240 millilitres)
- All-purpose flour (260 grams)
- Salt (5 grams)
- Canned sliced black olives (460 grams, chopped)
- Olive oil (30 millilitres)
- White sugar (20 grams)
- Dried thyme (5 grams)
- Dried onion (15 grams, minced)
- Bread machine yeast (6 grams)

Directions:

1. Place all ingredients in the baking pan of bread machine in the order recommended by manufacturer.
2. Place the baking pan in bread machine and close with lid.
3. Select "White Bread" setting.
4. Press start button.
5. Carefully remove the baking pan from machine and then invert the bread loaf onto a wire rack to cool completely before slicing.
6. Cut the bread loaf into desired-sized slices and serve.

Celery Bread

Servings|12   Time|3 hours 10 minutes

Nutritional Content (per serving):

Cal| 167   Fat| 3.4g   Protein| 5g   Carbs| 29g   Fibre| 1.6g

Ingredients:

- Canned cream of celery soup (630 millilitres)
- Canola oil (15 millilitres)
- Fresh celery leaves (10 grams, chopped)
- Bread flour (405 grams)
- Quick-cooking oats (45 grams)
- Ground ginger (1¼ grams)
- Active dry yeast (7 grams)
- Whole milk (45 millilitres, warm)
- Celery stalk (75 grams, chopped finely)
- Large egg (1, beaten)
- White sugar (5 grams)
- Celery salt (5 grams)
- Vital wheat gluten (30 grams)
- Celery seeds (10 grams)

Directions:

1. Place all ingredients in the baking pan of bread machine in the order recommended by manufacturer.
2. Place the baking pan in bread machine and close with lid.
3. Select "White Bread" setting.
4. Press start button.
5. Carefully remove the baking pan from machine and then invert the bread loaf onto a wire rack to cool completely before slicing.
6. Cut the bread loaf into desired-sized slices and serve.

Tomato & Onion Bread

Servings|12   Time|3 hours 10 minutes

Nutritional Content (per serving):

Cal| 131   Fat| 1.3g   Protein| 3.9g   Carbs| 25.8g   Fibre| 1.8g

Ingredients:

- Water (240 millilitres)
- Bread flour (320 grams)
- White sugar (10 grams)
- Salt (5 grams)
- Sun-dried tomatoes (15 grams, chopped finely)
- Garlic cloves (3, minced)
- Olive oil (10 millilitres)
- Whole-wheat flour (85 grams)
- Dried rosemary (5 grams)
- Active dry yeast (3 grams)
- Onion (10 grams, chopped finely)

Directions:

1. Place all ingredients except tomatoes, garlic and onion in the baking pan of bread machine in the order recommended by manufacturer.
2. Place the baking pan in bread machine and close with lid.
3. Select "White Bread" setting.
4. Press start button.
5. Carefully remove the baking pan from machine and then invert the bread loaf onto a wire rack to cool completely before slicing.
6. Cut the bread loaf into desired-sized slices and serve.

Parmesan Garlic Bread

Servings|12   Time|3 hours 55 minutes

Nutritional Content (per serving):

Cal| 241   Fat| 10.6g   Protein| 5.4g   Carbs| 31.5g   Fibre| 1.2g

Ingredients:

- Water (330 millilitres)
- Unsalted butter (55 grams, melted)
- Parmesan cheese (55 grams, grated)
- Dried basil (5 grams)
- White sugar (40 grams)
- Olive oil (60 millilitres)
- Garlic (5 grams, minced)
- All-purpose flour (425 grams)
- Garlic powder (2½ grams)
- Dried oregano (5 grams)
- Salt (10 grams)
- Active dry yeast (7 grams)

Directions:

1. Place all ingredients in the baking pan of bread machine in the order recommended by manufacturer.
2. Place the baking pan in bread machine and close with lid.
3. Select "Basic" setting and then "Medium Crust".
4. Press start button.
5. Carefully remove the baking pan from machine and then invert the bread loaf onto a wire rack to cool for 12-15 minutes before slicing.
6. Cut the bread loaf into desired-sized slices and serve warm.

Cheddar & Parmesan Bread

Servings|12   Time|3 hours 10 minutes

Nutritional Content (per serving):

Cal| 197   Fat| 6.5g   Protein| 7.9g   Carbs| 26.3g   Fibre| 1g

Ingredients:

- Water (300 millilitres)
- Bread flour (405 grams)
- Unsalted butter (15 grams, softened)
- Salt (5 grams)
- Active dry yeast (7 grams)
- Parmesan cheese (40 grams, grated)
- Water (300 millilitres)
- White sugar (25 grams)
- Bread flour (405 grams)
- White sugar (25 grams)
- Ground black pepper (2½ grams)
- Sharp cheddar cheese (170 grams, grated)

Directions:

1. Place all ingredients in the baking pan of bread machine in the order recommended by manufacturer.
2. Place the baking pan in bread machine and close with lid.
3. Select "White Bread" setting.
4. Press start button.
5. Carefully remove the baking pan from machine and then invert the bread loaf onto a wire rack to cool for 12-15 minutes before slicing.
6. Cut the bread loaf into desired-sized slices and serve warm.

Ricotta Bread

Servings|12   Time|3 hours 10 minutes

Nutritional Content (per serving):

Cal| 206   Fat| 5.6g   Protein| 8.3g   Carbs| 30.5g   Fibre| 1g

Ingredients:

- Ricotta cheese (425 grams)
- Unsalted butter (30 grams, melted and cooled)
- White sugar (50 grams)
- Active dry yeast (7½ grams)
- Whole milk (60 millilitres)
- Large egg (1, beaten)
- Bread flour (405 grams)
- Salt (5 grams)

Directions:

1. Place all ingredients in the baking pan of bread machine in the order recommended by manufacturer.
2. Place the baking pan in bread machine and close with lid.
3. Select "Basic" setting.
4. Press start button.
5. Carefully remove the baking pan from machine and then invert the bread loaf onto a wire rack to cool for 12-15 minutes before slicing.
6. Cut the bread loaf into desired-sized slices and serve warm.

Cheddar Green Onion Bread

Servings|16   Time|3 hours 10 minutes

Nutritional Content (per serving):

Cal| 192   Fat| 6.9g   Protein| 7g   Carbs| 25g   Fibre| 1g

Ingredients:

- Whole milk (60 millilitres)
- Water (60 millilitres)
- Unsalted butter (40 grams, softened)
- White sugar (10 grams)
- Salt (5 grams)
- Extra-sharp cheddar cheese (185 grams, shredded)
- Large egg (1, beaten)
- Bread flour (540 grams)
- Green onion (1 (green part), chopped finely)
- Active dry yeast (3¾ grams)

Directions:

1. Place all ingredients in the baking pan of bread machine in the order recommended by manufacturer.
2. Place the baking pan in bread machine and close with lid.
3. Select "Basic" setting.
4. Press the start button.
5. Carefully remove the baking pan from machine and then invert the bread loaf onto a wire rack to cool for 12-15 minutes before slicing.
6. Cut the bread loaf into desired-sized slices and serve warm.

Feta Olives Bread

Servings|12   Time|3 hours 10 minutes

Nutritional Content (per serving):

Cal| 152   Fat| 2.8g   Protein| 4.8g   Carbs| 26.6g   Fibre| 1.2g

Ingredients:

- Buttermilk (240 millilitres, warm)
- Olive oil (10 millilitres)
- White sugar (15 grams)
- Black olives (90 grams, halved and pitted)
- Feta cheese (40 grams, crumbled)
- Bread flour (405 grams)
- Salt (5 grams)
- Bread machine yeast (6 grams)

Directions:

1. Place all ingredients except for olives in the baking pan of bread machine in the order recommended by manufacturer.
2. Place the baking pan in bread machine and close with lid.
3. Select "Basic" setting.
4. Press start button.
5. Wait for bread machine to beep before adding the olives.
6. Carefully remove the baking pan from machine and then invert the bread loaf onto a wire rack to cool for at least 12-15 minutes before slicing.
7. Cut the bread loaf into desired-sized slices and serve warm.

Buns, Breadsticks & Muffins Recipes

Simple Buns

Servings|8   Time|2 hours 8 minutes

Nutritional Content (per serving):

Cal| 299   Fat| 8.4g   Protein| 7.1g   Carbs| 48.6g   Fibre| 1.8g

Ingredients:

- Water (240 millilitres, lukewarm)
- Large egg (1)
- White sugar (50 grams)
- Unsalted butter (40 grams, melted)
- Margarine (30 grams, softened)
- Large egg (1)
- All-purpose flour (425 grams)
- Salt (5 grams)
- Instant yeast (9 grams)

Directions:

1. For dough: place all ingredients except for butter in the baking pan of bread machine in the order recommended by manufacturer.
2. Place the baking pan in bread machine and close with lid.
3. Select "Dough" cycle and press start button.
4. After "Dough" cycle completes, remove the dough from bread pan.
5. With a plastic wrap, cover the dough for 1-2 hours or until doubled in size.
6. Place the dough onto lightly floured surface and with your hands, punch down it slightly.
7. Divide the dough into 8 portions and then, shape each into a ball.
8. Arrange the dough balls onto a lightly greased baking sheet in a single layer.
9. With a plastic wrap, cover the dough for 1 hour or until doubled in size.
10. Preheat your oven to 190 degrees C.
11. Remove the plastic wrap and brush the buns with half of melted butter.
12. Bake for approximately 15-18 minutes or until golden brown.
13. Remove the baking sheet from the oven and brush the buns with remaining melted Unsalted butter.
14. Place the baking sheet onto a wire rack to cool slightly before serving.

Whole-Wheat Buns

Servings|20   Time|2 hours 20 minutes

Nutritional Content (per serving):

Cal| 155   Fat| 5.5g   Protein| 3.8g   Carbs| 22.3g   Fibre| 0.8g

Ingredients:

- Whole milk (240 millilitres, warm)
- White sugar (50 grams)
- Salt (5 grams)
- All-purpose flour (130 grams)
- Unsalted butter (115 grams, softened)
- Medium eggs (2)
- Whole-wheat flour (390 grams)
- Instant yeast (9 grams)

Directions:

1. Place all ingredients in the baking pan of bread machine in the order recommended by manufacturer.
2. Place the baking pan in bread machine and close with lid.
3. Select "Dough" cycle and press start button.
4. After "Dough" cycle completes, remove the dough from bread pan.
5. Divide the dough into 20 portions and then, shape each into a ball.
6. Arrange the dough balls onto a lightly greased baking sheet in a single layer.
7. With a plastic wrap, cover the dough for 30-45 minutes or until doubled in size.
8. Preheat your oven to 180 degrees C.
9. Bake for approximately 20 minutes or until golden brown.
10. Remove the baking sheet from oven and place onto a wire rack to cool completely before serving.

Milky Buns

Servings|8   Time|2 hours 7 minutes

Nutritional Content (per serving):

Cal| 191   Fat| 4.2g   Protein| 5.6g   Carbs| 32.3g   Fibre| 1.2g

Ingredients:

- ❖ Large egg (1)
- ❖ Water (60 millilitres)
- ❖ White sugar (15 grams)
- ❖ Bread machine yeast (3¾ grams)
- ❖ Whole milk (120 millilitres)
- ❖ Unsalted butter (30 grams, softened)
- ❖ Salt (5 grams)
- ❖ All-purpose flour (325 grams)

Directions:

1. Place all ingredients in the baking pan of bread machine in the order recommended by manufacturer.
2. Place the baking pan in bread machine and close with lid.
3. Select "Dough" cycle and press start button.
4. After "Dough" cycle completes, remove the dough from bread pan place onto lightly floured surface.
5. Divide dough into 8 portions and then, shape each into a ball.
6. Arrange the buns onto a parchment paper-lined baking sheet in a single layer.
7. With a plastic wrap, cover the baking sheet and place in a warm place for 30-35 minutes or until doubled in size.
8. Preheat your oven to 200 degrees C.
9. Bake for approximately 10-12 minutes or until golden brown.
10. Remove the baking sheet from oven and place onto a wire rack to cool completely before serving.

Buttered Buns

Servings|20   Time|2 hours 6 minutes

Nutritional Content (per serving):

Cal| 129   Fat| 4.6g   Protein| 3.1g   Carbs| 18.7g   Fibre| 0.6g

Ingredients:

- ❖ Whole milk (240 millilitres, warm)
- ❖ White sugar (50 grams)
- ❖ Salt (7½ grams)
- ❖ Active dry yeast (7 grams)
- ❖ Unsalted butter (115 grams, softened)
- ❖ Medium eggs (2, beaten)
- ❖ Bread flour (540 grams)

Directions:

1. Place all ingredients in the baking pan of bread machine in the order recommended by manufacturer.
2. Place the baking pan in bread machine and close with lid.
3. Select "Dough" cycle and press start button.
4. After "Dough" cycle completes, remove the dough from bread pan and place onto a lightly floured surface.
5. Divide dough into 24 small portions and then, shape each into a ball.
6. Arrange the buns onto 2 lightly greased baking sheets in a single layer.
7. With a plastic wrap, cover each baking sheet and place in a warm place for 30-45 minutes or until doubled in size.
8. Preheat your oven to 180 degrees C.
9. Bake for approximately 13-16 minutes or until golden brown.
10. Remove the baking sheets from oven and place onto a wire rack to cool completely before serving.

Cinnamon Buns

Servings|12   Time|2¼ hours

Nutritional Content (per serving):

Cal| 196   Fat| 4.9g   Protein| 5.2g   Carbs| 32.5g   Fibre| 1.1g

Ingredients:

- Whole milk (240 millilitres)
- Large egg (1, beaten)
- All-purpose flour (440 grams)
- Salt (5 grams)
- Water (45 millilitres)
- Unsalted butter (55 grams)
- White sugar (40 grams)
- Dry yeast (6 grams)

Directions:

1. Place all ingredients in the baking pan of bread machine in the order recommended by manufacturer.
2. Place the baking pan in bread machine and close with lid.
3. Select "Dough" cycle and press start button.
4. After "Dough" cycle completes, remove the dough from bread pan and place onto a lightly floured surface.
5. With your hands, knead the dough until elastic.
6. With a floured rolling pin, roll the dough into ¼-inch thickness.
7. For filling: in a bowl, mix together all ingredients.
8. With a spoon, spread the filling on top of dough evenly.
9. Roll up dough to secure the filling.
10. Cut the dough into 1-inch thick circles.
11. Arrange the dough circles onto a greased baking sheet in a single layer.
12. With a tea towel, cover the baking sheet and place in a warm place for 30 minutes or until doubled in size.
13. Preheat your oven to 180 degrees C.
14. Bake for approximately 25 minutes or until golden brown.
15. Remove the baking sheet from oven and place onto a wire rack to cool completely before serving.

Honey Buns

Servings|20 Time|2¼ hours

Nutritional Content (per serving):

Cal| 139   Fat| 4.5g   Protein| 3g   Carbs| 18.5g   Fibre| 0.7g

Ingredients:

- ❖ Whole milk (240 millilitres, lukewarm)
- ❖ Honey (40 grams)
- ❖ Salt (5 grams)
- ❖ Canola oil (60 millilitres)
- ❖ Medium eggs (2)
- ❖ Bread flour (470 grams)
- ❖ Active dry yeast (7 grams)

Directions:

1. For dough: place all ingredients in the baking pan of bread machine in the order recommended by manufacturer.
2. Place the baking pan in bread machine and close with lid.
3. Select "Dough" cycle and press start button.
4. After "Dough" cycle completes, remove the dough from bread pan and place onto lightly floured surface.
5. Divide the dough into 20 portions and then, shape each into a ball.
6. Arrange the dough balls onto a lightly greased baking sheet in a single layer.
7. With a plastic wrap, cover the baking sheet and place in a warm place for 25-30 minutes or until doubled in size.
8. Preheat your oven to 180 degrees C.
9. Bake for approximately 20-25 minutes or until golden brown.
10. Remove the baking sheet from oven and place onto a wire rack to cool slightly before serving.

Cherries Buns

Servings|24   Time|2 hours 35 minutes

Nutritional Content (per serving):

Cal| 153   Fat| 4.6g   Protein| 3.4g   Carbs| 24.6g   Fibre| 3.4g

Ingredients:

- Active dry yeast (7 grams)
- All-purpose flour (585 grams)
- White sugar (100 grams)
- Whole milk (300 millilitres, lukewarm)
- Large egg (1)
- Water (60 millilitres)
- Salt (1¼ grams)
- Ground cardamom (5 grams)
- Unsalted butter (115 grams, melted)
- Dried cherries (80 grams)

Directions:

1. For dough: in a bowl place the Warm water and sprinkle with yeast.
2. Set aside for about 5 minutes until dissolved.
3. Place remaining dough ingredients except for cherries in the baking pan of bread machine in the order recommended by manufacturer and top with the yeast mixture.
4. Place the baking pan in bread machine and close with lid.
5. Select "Dough" cycle and press start button.
6. Wait for bread machine to beep before adding the cherries.
7. After "Dough" cycle completes, remove the dough from bread pan and place onto lightly floured surface.
8. Divide the dough into 24 portions and then, shape each into a ball.
9. Arrange the buns onto 2 lightly greased baking sheet in a single layer.
10. With a plastic wrap, cover each baking sheet and place in a warm place for 45 minutes or until doubled in size.
11. Preheat your oven to 180 degrees C.
12. Bake for approximately 20-25 minutes or until golden brown.
13. Remove the baking sheet from oven and place onto a wire rack to cool completely before serving.

Brioche Buns

Servings|16   Time|2 hours 10 minutes

Nutritional Content (per serving):

Cal| 140   Fat| 4.2g   Protein| 3.5g   Carbs| 22g   Fibre| 1g

Ingredients:

- Water (240 millilitres)
- Active dry yeast (9 grams)
- Large egg (1)
- Whole-wheat flour (50 grams)
- Unsalted butter (30 grams, softened)
- Whole milk (45 millilitres)
- White sugar (30 grams)
- Bread flour (405 grams)
- Salt (5 grams)
- Olive oil (30 millilitres)

Directions:

1. Place all ingredients except for oil in the baking pan of bread machine in the order recommended by manufacturer.
2. Place the baking pan in bread machine and close with lid.
3. Select "Dough" cycle and press start button.
4. Preheat your oven to 170 F, then turn it off.
5. After "Dough" cycle completes, remove the dough from bread pan and place onto lightly floured surface.
6. Divide the dough into 16 portions and then, shape each into a ball.
7. Arrange the buns onto 2 lightly greased baking sheets in a single layer.
8. With a kitchen towel, cover each baking sheet and place in the oven for 40 minutes.
9. In a shallow baking dish, place (120 millilitres) of water and arrange in the bottom of oven.
10. Remove the towel from the top of each baking sheet and set the temperature of oven to 200 degrees C.
11. Bake for approximately 15-20 minutes or until golden brown.
12. Remove the baking sheets from oven and immediately, brush the buns with olive oil.
13. Place the baking sheets onto a wire rack to cool completely before serving.

Cheddar & Cream Buns

Servings|16   Time|2 hours 12 minutes
Nutritional Content (per serving):
Cal| 190   Fat| 8.7g   Protein| 7g   Carbs| 20.6g   Fibre| 0.7g

Ingredients:

- Whole milk (240 millilitres, divided)
- Large egg (1)
- White sugar (30 grams)
- Bread machine yeast (6 grams)
- Cheddar cheese (230 grams, shredded)
- All-purpose flour (390 grams, divided)
- Heavy cream (15 grams)
- Salt (5 grams)
- Unsalted butter (55 grams, softened)

Directions:

1. In a microwave-safe bowl, add 120 millilitres of milk and (25 grams) of flour and microwave on High for 1¼ minute, stirring after every 30 seconds.
2. Add the remaining milk and beat vigorously until well combined.
3. Transfer the milk mixture into the bread machine pan.
4. Place the remaining flour and ingredients except for cheese in the baking pan of bread machine in the order recommended by manufacturer.
5. Place the baking pan in bread machine and close with lid.
6. Select "Dough" cycle and press start button.
7. After "Dough" cycle completes, remove the dough from bread pan and place onto lightly floured surface.
8. Divide the dough into 2 portions and shape each into a ball.
9. Place each dough ball onto a floured surface and with a rolling pin, roll it into a 13x9-inch rectangle.
10. Place the cheese on the top of each rectangle evenly.
11. Divide each rectangle into 4 equal-sized strips.
12. Then, divide each strip in half short-ways.
13. Starting from short ends, roll each strip.
14. Arrange the dough rolls onto 2 lightly greased baking sheets in a single layer.
15. With a plastic wrap, cover each baking sheet and place in a warm place until doubled in size.
16. Preheat your oven to 190 degrees C. Arrange a rack the middle shelf of oven.
17. Bake for approximately 10-15 minutes or until golden brown.
18. Remove the baking sheet from oven and place onto a wire rack to cool slightly before serving.

Swiss Cheese Buns

Servings|8   Time|2 hours 8 minutes

Nutritional Content (per serving):

Cal| 306   Fat| 8.2g   Protein| 8.9g   Carbs| 49g   Fibre| 1.8g

Ingredients:

- Water (240 millilitres, hot)
- Large egg (1, beaten)
- White sugar (50 grams)
- Instant yeast (9 grams)
- Swiss cheese (55 grams, grated)
- Unsalted butter (30 grams, softened)
- All-purpose flour (455 grams)
- Unsalted butter (20 grams, melted)

Directions:

1. Place all ingredients except for melted butter and cheese in the baking pan of bread machine in the order recommended by manufacturer.
2. Place the baking pan in bread machine and close with lid.
3. Select "Dough" cycle and press start button.
4. After "Dough" cycle completes, remove the dough from bread pan and place onto a lightly floured surface.
5. With your hands, punch down the dough to remove air bubbles.
6. Divide the dough into 8 portions and then, shape each into a ball.
7. Arrange the buns onto a parchment paper-lined baking sheet in a single layer.
8. With a plastic wrap, cover the baking sheet and place in a warm place for 1 hour or doubled in size.
9. Preheat your oven to 190 degrees C.
10. Brush each ball with melted butter.
11. Bake for approximately 12 minutes.
12. Open the oven and immediately, sprinkle each bun with cheese evenly.
13. Bake for approximately 6 minutes.
14. Remove the baking sheet from oven and place onto a wire rack to cool completely before serving.

Simple Breadsticks

Servings|12   Time|1 hour 57 minutes

Nutritional Content (per serving):

Cal| 103   Fat| 1.6g   Protein| 2.8g   Carbs| 19.1g   Fibre| 0.7g

Ingredients:

- Water (180 millilitres)
- White sugar (15 grams)
- Salt (5 grams)
- Dry yeast (3½ grams)
- Whole milk (15 millilitres)
- Unsalted butter (15 grams, cut into small chunks)
- Bread flour (305 grams)
- Large egg yolk (1)

Directions:

1. For dough: place all ingredients except for egg yolk and milk in the baking pan of bread machine in the order recommended by manufacturer.
2. Place the baking pan in bread machine and close with lid.
3. Select "Dough" cycle and press start button.
4. After "Dough" cycle completes, remove the dough from bread pan and place onto lightly floured surface.
5. Roll the dough into ¾-inch thickness.
6. Cut the dough into ¾-inch vertical strips.
7. Gently, press the cut side into the flour and arrange onto a lightly greased baking sheet in a single layer.
8. With a plastic wrap, cover the baking sheet and set aside in a warm place for about 20-30 minutes.
9. Preheat oven to 200 degrees C.
10. For egg wash: in a small bowl, add egg yolk and milk and beat lightly.
11. Remove the plastic wrap and brush the strips with egg wash.
12. Bake for approximately 10-12 minutes or until golden brown.
13. Serve warm.

Whole-Wheat Breadsticks

Servings|16   Time|2 hours 5 minutes

Nutritional Content (per serving):

Cal| 121   Fat| 3.4g   Protein| 2.7g   Carbs| 19.8g   Fibre| 0.8g

Ingredients:

- Water (240 millilitres, warm)
- Salt (5 grams)
- Whole-wheat flour (390 grams)
- Olive oil (60 millilitres)
- Brown sugar (45 grams)
- Active dry yeast (7½ grams)

Directions:

1. Place all ingredients in the baking pan of bread machine in the order recommended by manufacturer.
2. Place the baking pan in bread machine and close with lid.
3. Select "Dough" cycle and press start button.
4. After "Dough" cycle completes, remove the dough from bread pan and place onto lightly floured surface.
5. Roll the dough into a large rectangle and Cut the dough into 20 strips.
6. Arrange the strips onto 2 greased baking sheets in a single layer.
7. With a kitchen towel, cover the baking sheet and set aside in a warm place for about 1 hour.
8. Preheat oven to 190 degrees C.
9. Remove the kitchen towel and Bake for approximately 13-15 minutes or until golden brown.
10. Serve warm.

Sesame Seed Breadsticks

Servings|18   Time|2 hours

Nutritional Content (per serving):

Cal| 145   Fat| 3.2g   Protein| 3.8g   Carbs| 25.1g   Fibre| 1.1g

Ingredients:

- Water (330 millilitres, warm)
- Bread flour (540 grams)
- Salt (10 grams)
- Sesame seeds (40 grams)
- Active dry yeast (7½ grams)
- Unsalted butter (40 grams, softened)
- White sugar (50 grams)
- Dry milk powder (30 grams)

Directions:

1. Place all ingredients in the baking pan of bread machine in the order recommended by manufacturer.
2. Place the baking pan in bread machine and close with lid.
3. Select "Dough" cycle and press start button.
4. Preheat oven to 190 degrees C.
5. After "Dough" cycle completes, remove the dough from bread pan and place onto lightly greased surface.
6. Cut the dough into 18 strips.
7. Arrange the strips onto 2 greased baking sheets in a single layer.
8. Bake for approximately 10-15 minutes or until golden brown.
9. Serve warm.

Brown Sugar Breadsticks

Servings|24   Time|2 hours

Nutritional Content (per serving):

Cal| 80   Fat| 2.3g   Protein| 1.8g   Carbs| 13.2g   Fibre| 0.5g

Ingredients:

- Water (240 millilitres, warm)
- Salt (5 grams)
- Bread flour (405 grams)
- Brown sugar (40 grams)
- Olive oil (60 millilitres)
- Dry yeast (7½ grams)

Directions:

1. Place all ingredients in the baking pan of bread machine in the order recommended by manufacturer.
2. Place the baking pan in bread machine and close with lid.
3. Select "Dough" cycle and press start button.
4. After "Dough" cycle completes, remove the dough from bread pan and place onto lightly floured surface.
5. Roll the dough into a 10×12-inch rectangle and Cut the dough into strips.
6. Arrange the strips onto 2 greased baking sheets.
7. With a plastic wrap, cover each baking sheet and set aside in a warm place for about 20-25 minutes.
8. Preheat your oven to 190 degrees C.
9. Bake for approximately 10-15 minutes or until golden brown.
10. Serve warm.

Buttered Breadsticks

Servings|16   Time|2 hours 2 minutes

Nutritional Content (per serving):

Cal| 130   Fat| 4.6g   Protein| 2.5g   Carbs| 19.5g   Fibre| 0.7g

Ingredients:

- Water (255 millilitres, warm)
- Salt (7½ grams)
- Bread flour (405 grams)
- Salted butter (30 grams, melted)
- White sugar (25 grams)
- Unsalted butter (55 grams, softened)
- Active dry yeast (2¼ grams)

Directions:

1. Place all ingredients except for melted butter in the baking pan of bread machine in the order recommended by manufacturer.
2. Place the baking pan in bread machine and close with lid.
3. Select "Dough" cycle and press start button.
4. After "Dough" cycle completes, remove the dough from bread pan and place onto lightly floured surface.
5. Roll the dough into a rectangle and Cut the dough into strips.
6. Arrange the strips onto 2 parchment paper-lined baking sheets.
7. With a plastic wrap, cover each baking sheet and set aside in a warm place for about 20-25 minutes.
8. Preheat your oven to 200 degrees C.
9. Bake for approximately 12 minutes or until golden brown.
10. Remove from the oven and immediately brush breadsticks with melted butter.
11. Serve warm.

Honey Breadsticks

Servings|20   Time|1 hour 57 minutes

Nutritional Content (per serving):

Cal| 121   Fat| 2g   Protein| 3.5g   Carbs| 22.8g   Fibre| 2.1g

Ingredients:

- Water (330 millilitres)
- Canola oil (30 millilitres)
- Bread flour (270 grams)
- Active dry yeast (9 grams)
- Honey (60 grams)
- Salt (7½ grams)
- Whole-wheat flour (260 grams)

Directions:

1. Place all ingredients in the baking pan of bread machine in the order recommended by manufacturer.
2. Place the baking pan in bread machine and close with lid.
3. Select "Dough" cycle and press start button.
4. After "Dough" cycle completes, remove the dough from bread pan and place onto lightly floured surface.
5. Roll the dough into a rectangle and Cut the dough into strips.
6. Arrange the strips onto 2 greased baking sheets in a single layer.
7. With a plastic wrap, cover each baking sheet and set aside in a warm place for about 30 minutes.
8. Preheat your oven to 190 degrees C.
9. Bake for approximately 10-12 minutes or until golden brown.
10. Serve warm.

Italian Seasoning Breadsticks

Servings|16   Time|2 hours 5 minutes

Nutritional Content (per serving):

Cal| 113   Fat| 2.5g   Protein| 2.7g   Carbs| 19.8g   Fibre| 0.8g

Ingredients:

- Water (240 millilitres, warm)
- Salt (7½ grams)
- All-purpose flour (390 grams)
- Italian seasoning (5 grams)
- Active dry yeast (7 grams)
- Unsalted butter (40 grams, softened)
- White sugar (25 grams)
- Garlic powder (5 grams)

Directions:

1. Place all ingredients in the baking pan of bread machine in the order recommended by manufacturer.
2. Place the baking pan in bread machine and close with lid.
3. Select "Dough" cycle and press start button.
4. After "Dough" cycle completes, remove the dough from bread pan and place onto lightly floured surface.
5. Divide dough in 2 portions and shape each into a ball.
6. Then, divide each ball into a rope.
7. Arrange the ropes onto a 2 lightly greased baking sheets in a single layer.
8. With a plastic wrap, cover each baking sheet and set aside in a warm place for about 20 minutes.
9. Preheat your oven to 180 degrees C.
10. Bake for approximately 15 minutes or until browned.
11. Serve warm.

Basil Parmesan Breadsticks

Servings|20   Time|2 hours 12 minutes

Nutritional Content (per serving):

Cal| 96   Fat| 2.4g   Protein| 2.5g   Carbs| 16g   Fibre| 0.6g

Ingredients:

- Water (270 millilitres)
- Parmesan cheese (20 grams, grated)
- Salt (7½ grams)
- Unsalted butter (15 grams, melted)
- Olive oil (30 millilitres)
- White sugar (25 grams)
- Garlic powder (15 grams)
- Fresh basil (5 grams, minced)
- Active dry yeast (6 grams)

Directions:

1. Place all ingredients except for melted butter in the baking pan of bread machine in the order recommended by manufacturer.
2. Place the baking pan in bread machine and close with lid.
3. Select "Dough" cycle and press start button.
4. After "Dough" cycle completes, remove the dough from bread pan and place onto lightly floured surface.
5. Divide the dough into 20 portions and shape each into a ball.
6. Then, roll each into a 9-inch rope.
7. Arrange the ropes onto 2 lightly greased baking sheets in a single layer.
8. With a plastic wrap, cover the baking sheet and set aside in a warm place for about 40 minutes.
9. Preheat your oven to 180 degrees C.
10. Bake for approximately 18-22 minutes or until golden brown.
11. Remove the baking sheets from oven and brush the breadsticks with melted butter.
12. Serve warm.

Monterrey Jack Breadsticks

Servings|24   Time|2 hours 2 minutes
Nutritional Content (per serving):
Cal| 80   Fat| 2.1g   Protein| 2.9g   Carbs| 12.2g   Fibre| 0.5g

Ingredients:

- Water (240 millilitres, warm)
- Bread flour (405 grams)
- Parmesan cheese (30 grams, grated)
- Cracked black pepper (2½ grams)
- Active dry yeast (3 grams)
- Large egg white (1)
- Vegetable oil (30 millilitres)
- Italian seasoning (5 grams, crushed)
- Salt (5 grams)
- Monterrey Jack cheese with jalapeño peppers (55 grams, shredded)
- Whole milk (30 millilitres)

Directions:

1. For dough: place all ingredients except for egg white and milk in the baking pan of bread machine in the order recommended by manufacturer.
2. Place the baking pan in bread machine and close with lid.
3. Select "Dough" cycle and press start button.
4. After "Dough" cycle completes, remove the dough from bread pan and with your hands, punch down it slightly.
5. With a plastic wrap, cover the dough for 10 minutes.
6. Preheat your oven to 200 degrees C.
7. Place the dough onto lightly floured surface and divide into three portions.
8. Roll each dough portion into a 14x10-inch rectangle.
9. Cut the dough into strips.
10. Twist 2 strips together several times and then press ends together.
11. Arrange the strips onto 2 lightly greased baking sheets in a single layer.
12. For egg wash: in a small bowl, mix together egg white and milk.
13. Brush the twisted strips with egg wash.
14. Bake for approximately 10-12 minutes or until golden brown.
15. Serve warm.

Prosciutto Breadsticks

Servings|20   Time|2 hours
Nutritional Content (per serving):
Cal| 144   Fat| 3.3g   Protein| 7.6g   Carbs| 20.7g   Fibre| 0.8g

Ingredients:

For Dough:
- Water (330 millilitres)
- Unsalted butter (15 grams, softened)
- White sugar (20 grams)
- Salt (7½ grams)
- Bread flour (540 grams)
- Active dry yeast (6 grams)

For Topping:
- Prosciutto (225 grams, cut into very thin slices)
- Parmesan cheese (55 grams, grated freshly)
- Large egg yolk (1)
- Water (30 millilitres)

Directions:

1. For dough: place all ingredients in the baking pan of bread machine in the order recommended by manufacturer.
2. Place the baking pan in bread machine and close with lid.
3. Select "Dough" cycle and press start button.
4. After "Dough" cycle completes, remove the dough from bread pan and place onto lightly floured surface.
5. Roll the dough into ¼-inch thickness.
6. With a plastic wrap, cover the dough for 25-30 minutes.
7. Preheat your oven to 200 degrees C.
8. Remove the plastic wrap and place the prosciutto slices onto the dough evenly.
9. Sprinkle the top with Parmesan cheese evenly.
10. Cut the dough into strips and then, twist each end in opposite directions to twist the toppings into the bread stick.
11. Arrange the strips onto 2 lightly greased baking sheets in a single layer.
12. For egg wash: in a small bowl, mix together egg yolk and water.
13. Brush the strips with egg wash.
14. Bake for approximately 8-10 minutes or until golden brown.
15. Serve warm.

Milk Powder English Muffins

Servings|12   Time|2 hours 32 minutes

Nutritional Content (per serving):

Cal| 146   Fat| 2.6g   Protein| 4.5g   Carbs| 25.6g   Fibre| 1g

Ingredients:

- Water (240 millilitres)
- Unsalted butter (30 grams)
- Salt (1¼ grams)
- All-purpose flour (390 grams)
- Dry milk powder (60 grams)
- Large egg (1, beaten)
- White sugar (10 grams)
- Dry yeast (4½ grams)

Directions:

1. Place all ingredients in the baking pan of bread machine in the order recommended by manufacturer.
2. Place the baking pan in bread machine and close with lid.
3. Select "Dough" cycle and press start button.
4. After "Dough" cycle completes, remove the dough from bread pan and place onto a cornmeal dusted surface.
5. With your hands, pat the dough into a ½-¾-inch thick rectangle.
6. Turn the dough rectangle to coat with cornmeal lightly.
7. Cut the dough into 12 rounds.
8. Arrange the dough rounds onto a lightly greased baking sheet in a single layer.
9. With a plastic wrap, cover the baking sheet and place in a warm place for 20-30 minutes or until doubled in size.
10. Heat a lightly greased non-stick skillet over medium-low heat and cook the muffins in 3 batches for about 6-7 minutes per side or until golden brown.
11. With a knife, split each muffin and serve warm.

Honey English Muffins

Servings|12   Time|2 hours 6 minutes

Nutritional Content (per serving):

Cal| 182   Fat| 2.5g   Protein| 4.9g   Carbs| 35.1g   Fibre| 2.1g

Ingredients:

- Water (300 millilitres, warm)
- Salt (2½ grams)
- Unsalted butter (30 grams, softened)
- Active dry yeast (9 grams)
- Bread flour (405 grams)
- Whole-wheat flour (100 grams)

Directions:

1. Place all ingredients in the baking pan of bread machine in the order recommended by manufacturer.
2. Place the baking pan in bread machine and close with lid.
3. Select "Dough" cycle and press start button.
4. After "Dough" cycle completes, remove the dough from bread pan and place onto a lightly floured surface.
5. Shape the dough into a 12-inch long log and then, cut it into 12 (1-inch) pieces.
6. Shape each dough piece into a circle and then lightly press it to form the muffin.
7. Arrange the dough circles onto a cornmeal dusted baking sheet in a single layer.
8. With a plastic wrap, cover the baking sheet and place in a warm place for 1 hour or until doubled in size.
9. Heat a non-stick skillet over medium-high heat and cook the muffins I 2 batches for about 4 minutes per side or until golden brown.
10. With a knife, split each muffin and serve warm.

Milky English Muffins

Servings|8   Time|2 hours 18 minutes

Nutritional Content (per serving):

Cal| 238   Fat| 6g   Protein| 6.9g   Carbs| 38.6g   Fibre| 1.4g

Ingredients:

- ❖ Whole milk (240 millilitres)
- ❖ Large egg (1, beaten)
- ❖ White sugar (10 grams)
- ❖ Dry yeast (4½ grams)
- ❖ Unsalted butter (40 grams)
- ❖ Salt (2½ grams)
- ❖ All-purpose flour (390 grams)

Directions:

1. Place all ingredients in the baking pan of bread machine in the order recommended by manufacturer.
2. Place the baking pan in bread machine and close with lid.
3. Select "Dough" cycle and press start button.
4. After "Dough" cycle completes, remove the dough from bread pan and place onto a cornmeal dusted surface.
5. With your hands, pat the dough into a ½-inch thick rectangle.
6. Turn the dough rectangle to coat with cornmeal lightly.
7. Cut the dough into 8 rounds and arrange onto a lightly greased baking sheet in a single layer.
8. With a plastic wrap, cover the baking sheet and place in a warm place for 30 minutes or until doubled in size.
9. Heat a lightly greased non-stick skillet over medium-low heat and cook the muffins in 2 batches for about 6-7 minutes per side or until golden brown.
10. With a knife, split each muffin and serve warm.

Raisin English Muffins

Servings|8   Time|2 hours 22 minute

Nutritional Content (per serving):

Cal| 294   Fat| 6.1g   Protein| 7.6g   Carbs| 53.3g   Fibre| 2.3g

Ingredients:

- Whole milk (240 millilitres)
- Large egg (1, beaten)
- White sugar (10 grams)
- Dry yeast (6 grams)
- Ground cinnamon (2½ grams)
- Ground nutmeg (2½ grams)
- Unsalted butter (40 grams)
- Salt (2½ grams)
- All-purpose flour (390 grams)
- Raisins (150 grams)
- Ground ginger (2½ grams)

Directions:

1. Place all ingredients except for raisins and spices in the baking pan of bread machine in the order recommended by manufacturer.
2. Place the baking pan in bread machine and close with lid.
3. Select "Dough" cycle and press start button.
4. Wait for bread machine to beep before adding the raisins and spices.
5. After "Dough" cycle completes, remove the dough from bread pan and place onto a cornmeal dusted surface.
6. With your hands, pat the dough into a ½-inch thick rectangle.
7. Turn the dough rectangle to coat with cornmeal lightly.
8. Cut the dough into 8 rounds.
9. Arrange the dough rounds onto a lightly greased baking sheet in a single layer.
10. With a plastic wrap, cover the baking sheet and place in a warm place for 30 minutes or until doubled in size.
11. Heat a lightly greased non-stick skillet over medium heat and cook the muffins in 2 batches for about 6-8 minutes per side or until golden brown.
12. With a knife, split each muffin and serve warm.

Buttermilk Muffins

Servings|12   Time|2 hours 10 minutes

Nutritional Content (per serving):

Cal| 265   Fat| 9.4g   Protein| 6.7g   Carbs| 38.4g   Fibre| 1.2g

Ingredients:

- Whole milk (240 millilitres)
- Salt (5 grams)
- Large eggs (2, beaten)
- Baking powder (12 grams)
- All-purpose flour (520 grams)
- Buttermilk (240 millilitres)
- White sugar (50 grams)
- Unsalted butter (115 grams, melted)

Directions:

1. Place all ingredients except for raisins and spices in the baking pan of bread machine in the order recommended by manufacturer.
2. Place the baking pan in bread machine and close with lid.
3. Select "Basic" setting and press start button.
4. Preheat your oven to 190 degrees C. Line 2 (12-cups) muffin tins with paper liners.
5. Carefully remove the baking pan from machine and place the dough into the prepared muffin cups.
6. Bake for approximately 20-25 minutes or until a toothpick inserted in the center comes out clean.
7. Remove the muffin tin from oven and place onto a wire rack to cool for about 10 minutes.
8. Carefully invert the muffins onto the wire rack to cool completely before serving.

Index

A

All-purpose flour, 30, 33, 38, 48, 49, 51, 52, 54, 57, 59, 74, 75, 78, 81, 87, 88, 89, 91, 93, 95, 96, 103, 107, 109, 110, 111
Almonds, 30
Amaranth flour, 53
Anise seeds, 58
applesauce, 18, 21

B

Baking powder, 30, 38, 49, 54, 59, 111
basil, 71, 75, 81, 104
black pepper, 77, 82, 105
Blackberry jelly, 43
Bread flour, 8, 13, 17, 18, 19, 20, 21, 22, 23, 24, 25, 26, 28, 31, 32, 34, 35, 36, 37, 39, 40, 41, 42, 43, 44, 45, 46, 47, 50, 52, 53, 55, 56, 58, 61, 62, 63, 64, 66, 67, 68, 69, 70, 71, 72, 73, 76, 77, 79, 80, 82, 83, 84, 85, 90, 92, 94, 97, 99, 100, 101, 102, 105,106, 108
Brown sugar, 13, 20, 21, 28, 34, 37, 38, 39, 47, 48, 55, 56, 62, 67, 98, 100
butter, 9, 11, 13, 15, 16, 17, 19, 21, 30, 31, 32, 34, 35, 36, 39, 40, 41, 43, 47, 49, 50, 51, 52, 54, 55, 56, 59, 60, 61, 63, 67, 72, 73, 76, 81, 82, 83, 84, 87, 88, 89, 90, 91, 93, 94, 95, 96, 97, 99, 101, 103, 104, 106, 107, 108, 109, 110, 111
Buttermilk, 42, 85, 111

C

Canola oil, 14, 25, 26, 37, 79, 92, 102
Caraway seeds, 20, 23, 52
Cashews, 45
Celery salt, 79
Celery seeds, 79
Celery stalk, 79
Chai tea powder, 52
cheddar cheese, 74, 82, 84
Cheddar cheese, 95
cherries, 93
chives, 76
chocolate chips, 54, 61, 62
cinnamon, 18, 19, 21, 34, 38, 39, 44, 47, 55, 56, 110
Cocoa powder, 20, 60
coffee granules, 20
corn flour, 58

Corn syrup, 20
cornmeal, 26, 107, 108, 109, 110
Cornstarch, 59
Courgette, 18, 38
cranberries, 48, 50, 51, 54
Curry powder, 66

D

Dates, 30
Dill weed, 67

E

egg, 8, 19, 25, 27, 31, 32, 35, 36, 39, 46, 52, 56, 58, 61, 75, 79, 83, 84, 87, 89, 91, 93, 94, 95, 96, 97, 105, 106, 107, 109, 110

F

Feta cheese, 85
flaxseeds, 16

G

Garlic, 70, 71, 73, 80, 81, 103, 104
Garlic powder, 71, 81, 103, 104
ginger, 47, 56, 79, 110

H

Heavy cream, 95
Honey, 17, 22, 26, 32, 33, 41, 46, 50, 51, 53, 63, 66, 92, 102, 108

I

Italian seasoning, 77, 103, 105

L

Lemon, 18, 36

M

Maple syrup, 42, 45
Margarine, 10, 20, 23, 28, 44, 58, 87

milk powder, 9, 10, 18, 21, 23, 27, 31, 32, 37, 42, 46, 47, 53, 55, 59, 63, 66, 67, 73, 99, 107
Millet, 26
Molasses, 22, 40, 56, 57
Monterrey Jack cheese, 105
Mozzarella cheese, 71
mustard, 57, 66, 67

N

nutmeg, 35, 36, 110

O

oats, 17, 33, 37, 63, 79
Olive oil, 22, 29, 33, 45, 57, 63, 64, 66, 68, 70, 71, 75, 77, 78, 80, 81, 85, 94, 98, 100, 104
olives, 78, 85
onion, 71, 72, 78, 80, 84
orange, 59
oregano, 75, 81

P

Parmesan cheese, 68, 70, 71, 81, 82, 104, 105, 106
parsley, 70
Pepperoni, 71
pineapple juice, 46
potato flakes, 69
Prosciutto, 106
pumpkin, 29, 47, 48

Q

Quinoa flour, 15

R

Raisins, 21, 23, 38, 44, 56, 110
raspberries, 52
Ricotta cheese, 83
rosemary, 68, 73, 75, 77, 80
Rye flour, 20, 52, 57

S

Salt, 8, 9, 10, 11, 12, 13, 14, 15, 17, 18, 19, 20, 21, 22, 23, 24, 25, 26, 27, 28, 29, 30, 31, 32, 33, 34, 35, 36, 37, 38, 39, 40, 41, 42, 43, 44, 45, 46, 47, 48, 49, 50, 51, 54, 55, 56, 58, 61, 62, 63, 64, 66, 67, 68, 69, 70, 71, 72, 73, 74, 75, 76, 77, 78, 80, 81, 82, 83, 84, 85, 87, 88, 89, 90, 91, 92, 93, 94, 95, 97, 98, 99, 100, 101, 102, 103, 104, 105, 106, 107, 108, 109, 110, 111
Self-rising flour, 60
Sesame seeds, 99
Sour cream, 49, 76
Soy flour, 16
Spelt flour, 14
Splenda, 16
Sun-dried tomatoes, 68, 80
Sunflower seeds, 63
Sweet potato, 55
Swiss cheese, 96

T

thyme, 73, 78

V

Vanilla extract, 30, 49, 52, 54, 55, 60
Vegetable oil, 8, 12, 27, 38, 42, 43, 46, 48, 53, 62, 69, 72, 105
vinegar, 20, 27

W

Walnuts, 31, 38, 48, 52
Water, 8, 9, 10, 12, 16, 17, 18, 20, 21, 22, 23, 24, 26, 27, 28, 29, 30, 31, 33, 34, 35, 36, 37, 40, 43, 44, 48, 50, 51, 52, 53, 55, 57, 58, 61, 62, 63, 64, 66, 67, 68, 69, 70, 71, 72, 73, 75, 76, 77, 78, 80, 81, 82, 84, 87, 89, 91, 93, 94, 96, 97, 98, 99, 100,101, 102, 103, 104, 105, 106, 107, 108
wheat gluten, 16, 22, 57, 79
White flour, 9, 15, 29
white pepper, 69
White rice flour, 27
White sugar, 9, 10, 11, 12, 14, 15, 18, 19, 23, 24, 27, 30, 31, 35, 36, 38, 39, 40, 43, 44, 49, 52, 54, 58, 59, 60, 61, 64, 68, 69, 70, 71, 72, 73, 74, 75, 76, 77, 78, 79, 80, 81, 82, 83, 84, 85, 87, 88, 89, 90, 91, 93, 94, 95, 96, 97, 99, 101, 103, 104, 106, 107, 109, 110, 111
Whole milk, 11, 13, 14, 15, 19, 27, 35, 39, 40, 41, 45, 49, 54, 56, 58, 60, 61, 68, 69, 74, 76, 79, 83, 84, 88, 89, 90, 91, 92, 93, 94, 95, 97, 105, 109, 110, 111
Whole-wheat flour, 10, 11, 12, 13, 22, 26, 28, 29, 37, 40, 42, 43, 48, 53, 57, 63, 66, 67, 80, 88, 94, 98, 102, 108

X

Xanthan gum, 27

Y

yeast, 8, 9, 10, 11, 12, 13, 14, 15, 16, 17, 18, 19, 20, 21, 22, 23, 24, 25, 26, 27, 28, 29, 31, 32, 33, 35, 36, 37, 39, 40, 41, 42, 43, 44, 45, 46, 47, 48, 50, 51, 52, 53, 55, 56, 57, 58, 61, 62, 63, 64, 66, 67, 68, 69, 70, 71, 72, 73, 74, 75, 76, 77, 78, 79, 80, 81, 82, 83, 84, 85, 87, 88, 89, 90, 91, 92, 93, 94, 95, 96, 97, 98, 99, 100, 101, 102, 103, 104, 105, 106, 107, 108, 109, 110

yoghurt, 11, 51

Printed in Great Britain
by Amazon